ADDITIONAL PRAISE FOR
MARSHALL ROSENBERG, PhD

"We should all be grateful to Marshall Rosenberg. He provides us with the most effective tools to foster health and relationships. Nonviolent Communication connects soul to soul, creating a lot of healing and helps us express honestly from the heart what are people doing that is or is not in harmony with our needs. NVC is the missing element in what we do."

—Deepak Chopra,
author of *Ageless Body, Timeless Mind*

"Dr. Rosenberg has brought the simplicity of successful communication into the foreground. No matter what issue you're facing, his strategies for communicating with others will set you up to win every time."

—Anthony Robbins,
author of *Awaken the Giant Within* and *Unlimited Power*

"Written with a profound level of clarity and compassion known only to those who practice what they preach, Marshall's *Living Nonviolent Communication* opens us to give our heart's willing consent to communicate in ways that foster authentic trust and intimate connection both with ourselves and in all forms of relationship."

—Michael Bernard Beckwith,
author of *Life Visioning: A Transformative Process
for Activating Your Unique Gifts and Highest Potential*

LIVING
Nonviolent
Communication

LIVING
Nonviolent
Communication

Practical Tools *to* Connect
and Communicate Skillfully
in Every Situation

MARSHALL
ROSENBERG, PhD

sounds true
BOULDER, COLORADO

Sounds True, Inc.
Boulder, CO 80306

Cover design by Jennifer Miles

Book design by Beth Skelley

Printed in the United States of America

Library of Congress Cataloging-in-Publication Data

Rosenberg, Marshall B.
Living nonviolent communication : practical tools to connect and communicate skillfully in every situation / Marshall B. Rosenberg.
p. cm.
ISBN 978-1-60407-787-2
1. Interpersonal communication. 2. Interpersonal conflict. 3. Conflict management. I. Title.
BF637.C45R644 2012
153.6—dc23
2011044907

eBook ISBN: 978-1-60407-827-5

10 9 8 7 6 5 4

CONTENTS

A Brief Introduction to Nonviolent Communication. vii

~ 1 WE CAN WORK IT OUT 1
    Resolving Conflicts Peacefully and Powerfully

2 BEING ME, LOVING YOU 19
    A Practical Guide to Extraordinary Relationships

3 GETTING PAST THE PAIN BETWEEN US 63
    Healing and Reconciliation without Compromise

~ 4 THE SURPRISING PURPOSE OF ANGER 95
    Beyond Anger Management—Finding the Gift

5 RAISING CHILDREN COMPASSIONATELY. 125
    Parenting the Nonviolent Communication Way

6 PRACTICAL SPIRITUALITY 143
    Reflections on the Spiritual Basis of Nonviolent Communication

RECOMMENDED READING 165

ABOUT THE CENTER FOR NONVIOLENT COMMUNICATION 167

ABOUT THE AUTHOR. 169

A Brief Introduction to
Nonviolent Communication

Nonviolent Communication, or NVC, is a powerful model of communication, but it goes far beyond that. It is a way of being, thinking, and living in the world. Its purpose is to inspire heartfelt connections between ourselves and other people—connections that allow everyone's needs to be met through compassionate giving. It inspires us and others to give from the heart. It also helps us connect to our inner divinity and to what is alive in us moment to moment.

We could say that NVC is a language of compassion, but it is really a language of life in which compassion comes naturally. The model shows us how to express what is alive in us and to see what is alive in other people. Once we get clear about what is alive in us, we can look at what we can do to enrich that life.

Nonviolent Communication evolved out of an intense interest I had in two questions. First, I wanted to better understand what happens to human beings that leads some of us to behave violently and exploitatively. And second, I wanted to better understand what kind of education serves our attempts to remain compassionate—which I believe is our nature—even when others are behaving violently or exploitatively. The theory that has been around for many centuries says that violence and exploitation

Some Basic Feelings We All Have

Feelings When Needs Are Fulfilled	Feelings When Needs Are Not Fulfilled
Amazed	Angry
Comfortable	Annoyed
Confident	Concerned
Eager	Confused
Energetic	Disappointed
Fulfilled	Discouraged
Glad	Distressed
Hopeful	Embarrassed
Inspired	Frustrated
Intrigued	Helpless
Joyous	Hopeless
Moved	Impatient
Optimistic	Irritated
Proud	Lonely
Relieved	Nervous
Stimulated	Overwhelmed
Surprised	Puzzled
Thankful	Reluctant
Touched	Sad
Trustful	Uncomfortable

happen because people are innately evil, selfish, or violent. But I have seen people who aren't like that; I have seen many people who enjoy contributing to one another's well-being. So, I wondered why some people seem to enjoy other people's suffering, while other people are just the opposite.

In my exploration of these two questions, I found that the following three factors are very important in understanding why some of us respond violently and some of us respond compassionately in similar situations:

- The language that we have been educated to use
- How we have been taught to think and communicate
- The specific strategies we have learned to influence others and ourselves

Some Basic Needs We All Have

Autonomy
Choosing one's dreams, goals, ·and values

Choosing one's plan for fulfilling thoses dreams, goals, and values

Celebration
Celebrating the creation of life and dreams fulfilled

Celebrating losses of loved ones, dreams, and so on (mourning)

Integrity
Authenticity

Creativity

Meaning

Self-worth

Interdependence
Acceptance

Appreciation

Closeness

Community

Consideration

Contributing to the enrichment of life (exercising one's power by giving that which contributes to life)

Emotional safety

Empathy

Honesty (the empowering honesty that enables us to learn from our limitations)

Love

Reassurance

Respect

Support

Trust

Understanding

Warmth

Physical Nurturance
Air

Food

Movement and exercise

Protection from life-threatening forms of life, such as viruses, bacteria, insects, predatory animals, and so on

Rest

Sexual expression

Shelter

Touch

Water

Play
Fun

Laughter

Spiritual Communion
Beauty

Harmony

Inspiration

Order

Peace

Because these three factors play a large role in determining whether we are able to respond compassionately or violently in situations, I have integrated the type of language, the kinds of thinking, and the forms of communication that strengthen our ability to willingly contribute to our own well-being and the well-being of others into this process that I call Nonviolent Communication.

The NVC process shows us how to nakedly express how we are and what is alive in us—without any criticism and without any analysis of others that implies wrongness. The process is based on the assumption that anything that people hear from us that sounds like an analysis or a criticism, or that implies wrongness on their part, prevents us from connecting with them in a way that allows everyone to contribute to one another's well-being. This approach to communication emphasizes compassion—rather than fear, guilt, shame, blame, coercion, or threat of punishment—as the motivation for action. In other words, it is about getting what we want for reasons that we will not regret later. Part of the process is to say clearly, without analysis, criticism, or blame, what is alive in us. Another part is to say clearly what would make life more wonderful for us and to present this information to others as requests and not as demands.

Nonviolent Communication focuses attention on whether people's needs are being fulfilled, and if they're not on what can be done to fulfill these needs. (See the introduction for the charts "Some Basic Feelings We All Have" and "Some Basic Needs We All Have.") It shows us how to express ourselves in ways that increase the likelihood that others will willingly contribute to our well-being. It also shows us how to receive the messages of others in ways that will increase the likelihood that we will willingly contribute to their well-being.

My hope is that the material in this book will help you communicate to others using this language of life and will show you how to hear this same quality of communication in the messages of others, regardless of how they speak.

The Four-Part Nonviolent Communication Process

Clearly expressing how I am without blaming or criticizing	Empathically receiving how you are without hearing blame or criticism
1. OBSERVATION	
What I observe (see, hear, remember, imagine, free from my evaluations) that does or does not contribute to my well-being: *"When I (see, hear) ..."*	What you observe (see, hear, remember, imagine, free from your evaluations) that does or does not contribute to your well-being: *"When you see/hear ..."* (Sometimes unspoken when offering empathy.)
2. FEELINGS	
How I feel (emotion or sensation rather than thought) in relation to what I observe: *"I feel ..."*	How you feel (emotion or sensation rather than thought) in relation to what you observe: *"You feel ..."*
3. NEEDS	
What I need or value (rather than a preference or a specific action) that causes my feelings: *"because I need/value ..."*	What you need or value (rather than a preference or a specific action) that causes your feelings: *"because you need/value ..."*
Clearly requesting that which would enrich my life without demanding	Empathically receiving that which would enrich your life without hearing any demand
4. REQUESTS	
The concrete actions I would like taken: *"Would you be willing to ...?"*	The concrete actions you would like taken: *"Would you like ...?"* (Sometimes unspoken when offering empathy.)

WE CAN WORK IT OUT

Resolving Conflicts
Peacefully and Powerfully

For more than forty years, I've mediated a wide variety of conflicts between parents and children, husbands and wives, management and workers, Palestinians and Israelis, Serbians and Croatians, and warring groups in Sierra Leone, Nigeria, Burundi, Sri Lanka, and Rwanda. What I've learned from dealing with conflicts at all these levels is that it is possible to resolve conflicts peacefully and to everyone's satisfaction. The likelihood of conflicts being resolved in this fulfilling way is significantly increased if a certain quality of human connection can be established between the parties in conflict.

I've developed a process called Nonviolent Communication (NVC), which consists of thought and communication skills that empower us to connect compassionately with others and ourselves. My colleagues and I are extremely pleased with the many different ways that people are using NVC in their personal lives, work settings, and political activities.

In the following pages, I describe how the Nonviolent Communication process supports efforts to resolve conflicts peacefully. The process can be used either when we ourselves are directly involved in conflict or when we are mediating the conflicts of others.

When I am called into a conflict resolution, I begin by guiding the participants to find a caring and respectful quality of connection among themselves. Only after this connection is present do I engage them in a search for strategies to resolve the conflict. At that time, we do not look for *compromise*; rather, we seek to resolve the conflict to everyone's complete satisfaction. To practice this process of conflict resolution, we must completely abandon the goal of *getting people to do what we want*. Instead, we focus on creating the conditions whereby *everyone's needs will be met*.

To further clarify this difference in focus (between getting what we want and getting what everyone wants), let's imagine that someone is behaving in a way that's not fulfilling a need of ours, and we make a request that the person behave differently. In my experience, that person will resist what we request if they see us as only interested in getting our own needs met and if they don't trust that we are equally concerned with meeting *their* needs. Genuine cooperation is inspired when participants trust that their own needs and values will be respectfully addressed. The Nonviolent Communication process is based on respectful practices that foster genuine cooperation.

USING NONVIOLENT COMMUNICATION TO RESOLVE CONFLICTS

The Nonviolent Communication practices that support conflict resolution involve

1. expressing our own needs;
2. sensing the needs of others, regardless of how others are expressing themselves;
3. checking to see whether needs are accurately being received;
4. providing the empathy people need in order to hear the needs of others; and
5. translating proposed solutions or strategies into positive action language.

Defining and Expressing Needs (Needs Are Not Strategies)

It has been my experience that if we keep our focus on needs, our conflicts tend toward a mutually satisfactory resolution. When keeping our focus on needs, we express our own needs, clearly understand the needs of others, and avoid any language that implies wrongness of the other party. On page ix, you can see a list of the basic human needs we all share.

Unfortunately, I've found that very few people are literate in expressing their needs. Instead they have been trained to criticize, insult, and otherwise communicate in ways that create distance among people. As a result, even in conflicts for which resolutions exist, resolutions are not found. Instead of both parties expressing their own needs and understanding the needs of the other party, both sides play the game of who's right. That game is more likely to end in various forms of verbal, psychological, or physical violence than in a peaceful resolution of differences.

Because needs are such a vital component of this approach to conflict resolution, I'd like to clarify what I'm referring to when I talk about needs. *Needs,* as I use the term, can be thought of as resources that life requires in order to sustain itself. For example, our physical well-being depends on our needs for air, water, rest, and food being fulfilled. Our psychological and spiritual well-being is enhanced when our needs for understanding, support, honesty, and meaning are fulfilled.

According to this definition of *needs,* regardless of our gender, educational level, religious beliefs, or nationality, all human beings have the same needs. What differs from person to person is the strategy for fulfilling needs. I've found that it facilitates conflict resolution to keep our needs separate from the strategies that might fulfill them.

One guideline for separating needs from strategies is to keep in mind that needs contain no reference to specific people taking specific action. In contrast, effective strategies—or what are more commonly referred to as wants, requests, desires, and "solutions"—*do* refer to specific people taking specific actions. An exchange between a husband and wife who had just about given up on their marriage will clarify this important difference between needs and strategies.

I asked the husband what needs of his were not being fulfilled in the marriage. He responded, "I need to get out of this relationship." Since he was talking about a specific person (himself) taking specific action (leaving the marriage), he was not expressing a need as I define it. Instead he was telling me a strategy that he was thinking of using. I pointed this out to him and suggested that we delay talking about strategies until we had really clarified both his needs and the needs of his wife. When they were able to clarify their needs, both saw that strategies other than ending the relationship could meet their needs. And I'm pleased to say that in the two years since that time, they've developed a relationship within the marriage that is very satisfactory to both.

Many people find it difficult to express needs. This lack of "need literacy" creates problems when people want to resolve conflicts. As an example, I would like to tell you about a husband and wife whose attempts to resolve conflicts led them to physical violence.

I had been working in the husband's workplace, offering some training. At the end of the training, the husband asked whether he could talk to me privately. He tearfully expressed the situation between his wife and himself and asked if I would meet with them to support them in resolving some of their conflicts. The wife agreed, and so I met with them that evening.

I began by saying, "I'm aware that you're both in a lot of pain. I would suggest that we begin with each of you expressing whatever needs of yours are not being fulfilled in the relationship. Once you understand one another's needs, I'm confident we can explore some strategies to meet those needs." What I was asking them required a literacy of expressing needs and an ability to understand one another's needs.

Unfortunately, they weren't able to do as I suggested. They didn't have the literacy. Instead of expressing his needs, the husband said, "The problem with you is that you're totally insensitive to my needs." Immediately his wife responded by saying, "That's typical of you to say unfair things like that."

Another time I was working within a company that had had a very disturbing conflict for more than fifteen months, and the conflict was creating morale as well as productivity problems. Within this conflict were two different factions from the same department. The conflict involved a debate over which piece of software to use, and strong emotions were involved. One faction had worked very hard to develop the software that was presently in use, and they wanted to continue its use. The other faction had strong emotions tied up in a new piece of software.

When I met with this group, I started in the same way as with the husband and wife. I asked both sides to tell me what needs of theirs would be better fulfilled by the software they advocated. As in the situation with the husband and wife, I didn't receive a clear expression of needs. Instead, each side responded with an intellectual analysis, which the other side received as criticism.

A member of one faction said, "I think that if we continue to be overly conservative we could be out of work in the future, because to be progressive requires that we take some risks and dare to show that we are beyond old-fashioned ways of doing things." A member of the other faction responded, "But I think that impulsively grabbing for every new thing that comes along is not in our best interest." They told me that they had been repeating these same analyses of one another for months and were getting nowhere. In fact, they were creating a lot of tension among themselves.

Like the husband and wife, they didn't know how to directly express their needs. Instead they were making analyses and were being heard by the other side as critical. This is how wars are created. When we're not able to say clearly what we need and only know how to make analyses of others that sound like criticism, wars are never far away, whether they are verbal, psychological, or physical.

Sensing the Needs of Others (No Matter How They Express Themselves)

The approach to conflict resolution that I am describing requires not only that we learn to express our needs, but also that we assist others in clarifying their needs. We can train ourselves to hear needs being expressed through the messages of others, regardless of how others are expressing themselves.

I've taught myself to do this because I believe that every message, whatever its form or content, is an expression of a need. If we accept this assumption, we can train ourselves to sense what needs might be at the root of any particular message. Thus, if I ask a question about what someone has just said, and that person responds, "That's a stupid question," I choose to sense what the other person might need as expressed through that particular judgment of me. For example, I might guess that a need for understanding was not being fulfilled when I asked that particular question. Or if I request that someone talk with me about some stress in our relationship, and the response is, "I don't want to talk about it," I might sense a need for protection from what that person imagines might happen if we communicate.

This ability to sense what people need is crucial in mediating conflicts. We can help by sensing what both sides need and putting it into words, and then we help each side hear the other side's needs. This creates a quality of connection that moves the conflict to successful resolution.

Let me give you an example of what I mean. I often work with groups of married couples. In these groups, I identify the couple with the most long-standing conflict, and I make a rather startling prediction to the group. I predict that we will be able to resolve this long-standing conflict within twenty minutes from the point at which both sides can tell me what the other side needs.

When I was doing this with one group, we identified a couple that had been married for thirty-nine years. They had a conflict about money. Six months into the marriage, the wife had twice overdrawn the checkbook, so the husband had taken control of the checkbook and wouldn't let her write checks from that point on. They had been arguing about this for thirty-nine years.

When the wife heard my prediction, she said, "Marshall, I can tell you this—that's not going to happen. I mean, we have a good marriage, we communicate quite well, but in this conflict we just have different needs about money. I don't see how it can possibly be resolved in twenty minutes."

I corrected her by saying that I hadn't predicted we'd resolve it in twenty minutes. "I predicted resolution within twenty minutes after both of you tell me what the other person needs." She said, "But Marshall, we communicate very well, and when you have been talking about something for thirty-nine years, you certainly understand what the other side needs."

I responded, "Well, I've been wrong before. I certainly could be wrong in this situation, but let's explore. Tell me—if you know what his needs are, what are they?"

She said, "It's very obvious, Marshall. He doesn't want me to spend any money."

The husband immediately reacted by saying, "That's ridiculous."

It was clear that she and I had a different definition of *needs*. When she said he didn't want her to spend any money, she was identifying what I call a strategy. Even if she were right, she would have been accurate about his desired *strategy* but not about his *need*. A need, as I define it, contains no reference to specific actions, such as spending money or not spending money.

I told her that all human beings have the same needs, and I was certain that if she could get clear about what her husband's needs were and if he were clear about her needs, we could resolve the issue. I said, "Can you try again? What do you think his need is?"

And she said, "Well, let me explain, Marshall. You see, he's just like his own father." And then she told me how her father-in-law was reluctant to spend money.

I stopped her and said, "Hold on, now. You're giving me an analysis of why he is the way he is. What I am asking is for you to simply tell me what need of his is involved in this situation. You're giving me an intellectual analysis of what has gone on in his life."

It was very clear that she didn't know how to identify his need. Even after thirty-nine years of talking, she still didn't have an idea of what his needs were. She had diagnoses of him, she had an intellectual awareness of what his reasons might be for not wanting her to have the checkbook, but she didn't really understand his needs in this situation.

So, I asked the husband, "Since your wife is not in touch with what your needs are, why don't you tell her? What needs of yours are being met by keeping the checkbook yourself?"

He said, "Marshall, she's a wonderful wife, a wonderful mother. But when it comes to money, she's totally irresponsible."

Again, notice the difference between the question I asked him, "What are your needs in this situation?" and his response. Instead of telling me what his needs were, he gave me a diagnosis that she was irresponsible. It's that kind of language that I believe gets in the way of resolving conflicts peacefully. At the point where either party hears themselves criticized, diagnosed, or intellectually interpreted, I predict their energy will turn toward self-defense and counteraccusations rather than toward resolutions that meet everyone's needs.

I pointed out to him that he was not really in touch with what his needs were, and I showed that he was giving me a diagnosis of his wife instead. Then I again asked him, "What are your needs in this situation?" He couldn't identify them.

Even after thirty-nine years of discussion, neither person was really aware of the other person's needs. Here was a situation in which my ability to sense needs could help them out of conflict. I used Nonviolent Communication skills to guess the needs that the husband and wife were expressing as judgments.

I reminded the husband that he had said his wife was totally irresponsible about money (a judgment), and then I asked, "Are you feeling scared in this situation because you have a need to protect the family economically?" When I said this, he looked at me and said, "That's exactly what I'm saying!" Of course, he hadn't been saying exactly that, but when we sense what people need, I believe that we're getting closer to the truth, closer to what they are trying to say. I believe that all analysis that implies wrongness is basically a tragic expression of unmet needs. If we can hear what people need, it's a great gift to them, because it helps them get connected to life.

Although I happened to guess right in this situation, it didn't require that I guess right. Even if I had been off, at least I was focusing his attention on needs. Focusing in this way helps people get more in touch with their needs. It takes them out of the analysis and gets them more connected to life.

Checking to See That Needs Are Accurately Received

Once he had expressed his need, the next step was to be sure that his wife had heard it. This is a crucial skill in conflict resolution. We can't assume that just because a message is expressed, the other person receives it accurately. Whenever I am mediating a conflict, if I am not sure that the people hearing the message have accurately received it, I ask them to repeat it back.

I asked his wife, "Could you tell me what you heard your husband's needs are in this situation?"

And she said, "Well, just because I overdrew the bank account a couple of times when we got married, that doesn't mean I'm going to continue doing it."

Her response was not atypical in my experience. When people have pain built up over many years, even when the other person clearly expresses a need, it doesn't mean the first person can hear it. Often, they're both so filled with their own pain that it gets in the way of their hearing one another.

I asked her if she could possibly repeat back what the husband had said, but it was clear that she really hadn't heard it, that she was in too much pain. I said to her, "I would like to tell you what I heard your husband say, and I would like you to repeat it back." I continued, "I heard your husband say that he has a need to protect the family. He's scared, because he really wants to be sure that the family is protected."

Providing Empathy to Heal the Pain (That Prevents People from Hearing One Other)

The wife still couldn't hear her husband's need, so I used another skill that is often necessary in conflict resolution—I shifted. Instead of trying to get her to repeat what he'd said, I tried to understand the pain that she felt.

I said, "I sense that you're feeling really hurt, and you need to be trusted so that you can learn from past experience." You could tell from her eyes that she really needed that understanding, and she said, "Yes, exactly."

Having received this understanding, I hoped that she would now be able to hear her husband, so once again I repeated what I understood his needs to be. He needed to protect the family. I asked her to repeat back what she heard. She replied, "So, he thinks I'm spending too much money."

As you see, she wasn't trained to hear needs any more than she was trained to express them. Instead of hearing his needs, all she heard was a diagnosis of herself. I suggested that she try to just hear the needs, without hearing any criticism of herself in it. After I repeated it two more times, she was finally able to hear her husband's needs.

Then I reversed the process and asked the wife to express her needs. Again, she wasn't able to do it directly; she expressed her need in the form of a judgment and said, "He doesn't trust me. He thinks I'm stupid and that I'm not going to be able to learn. I think that's unfair. I mean, just because I did it a couple of times doesn't mean I'll continue to do it."

Once again I loaned her the skill of my being able to sense her needs behind all of that. I said to her, "It sounds like you really have a need to be trusted. You really want acknowledgment that you can learn from the situation."

Then I asked the husband to tell me what his wife's needs were. And just as she had had judgments that kept her from hearing him at first, he couldn't hear her. He wanted to defend his need to protect the family and began to explain that she was a good wife, a good mother, but that she was just totally irresponsible when it came to money. I had to help him hear through his judgment, to just hear what her needs were, so I said, "Would you please just tell me what her needs are?" He had to have it repeated three times, but finally he heard her need was to be trusted.

As I had predicted, at the point when they both had heard each other's needs, it didn't take twenty minutes to find a way of getting everybody's needs met. It took much less time than that!

The more I have been involved in conflicts over the years and the more I've seen what leads families to argue or what leads nations to war, the more I believe that most schoolchildren could resolve these conflicts. If people just asked, "Here are the needs of both sides. Here are the resources. What can be done to meet these needs?" the conflict would be easy to resolve. But tragically, we're not taught to think in terms of the human needs involved, and our thinking does not go to that level. Instead it goes to dehumanizing one another with labels and judgments, and then even the simplest of conflicts becomes very difficult to solve.

Resolving Disputes Between Groups of People

To show how these same principles can apply when there are more than two people involved, let's examine a conflict that I was asked to mediate between two tribes in Nigeria. These tribes had had enormous violence going on between them for the previous year. In fact, one-fourth of their population had been killed—one hundred out of four hundred people dead—in one year.

Seeing this violence, a colleague of mine who lives in Nigeria had worked hard to get the chiefs on both sides to agree to meet with me to see if we could resolve the conflict. After much effort, he finally got them to agree.

As we were walking into the session, my colleague whispered to me, "Be prepared for a little bit of tension, Marshall. Three of the people in the room know that the person who killed their child is in that room." It was very tense at first. There had been so much violence between these two groups, and it was the first time they had really sat down together.

I started with the question with which I frequently start conflict resolution sessions in order to focus on people's needs. I said to both sides, "I'd like whoever would like to speak first to say what your needs are in this situation. After everyone understands the needs of everyone else, then we'll move to finding some ways of meeting the needs."

Unfortunately, like the husband and wife, they didn't have a literacy of needs—they only knew how to tell me what was wrong with the other side. Instead of responding to my question, the chief from one side looked across the table and said, "You people are murderers," and the other side responded, "You've been trying to dominate us. We're not going to tolerate it anymore!" We had more tension after two sentences than we had when I had walked in.

Obviously, getting people together to communicate doesn't help unless they know how to communicate in a way that connects them as human beings. My job was the same as it was with the married couple: lend them the ability to sense the needs behind whatever is being expressed.

I turned to the chief who had said "You people are murderers" and guessed, "Chief, do you have a need for safety and to be sure that whatever conflicts are going on will be resolved by some means other than violence?" The chief immediately said to me, "Of course, that's what I'm saying!" Well, of course, he hadn't said that. He'd said that the other person was a murderer and had made a judgment rather than expressing his needs. However, now we had his needs out on the table, so I turned to a chief from the other side and said, "Chief, would you please reflect back what he said his needs were?"

The chief responded to this man by asking in a very hostile way, "Then why did you kill my son?"

That started an uproar between the two groups. After things calmed down, I said, "Chief, we'll deal with your reaction to his needs later, but at the moment, I suggest that you just hear his needs. Could you repeat back what he said his needs were?" He couldn't do it. He was so emotionally involved in this situation and in his judgments of the other person that he didn't hear what the other person's needs were. I repeated the needs as I had heard them and said, "Chief, I heard the other chief saying that he has a need for safety. He has a need to feel secure—that no matter what conflicts are present, they'll be resolved in some way other than by violence. Could you just reflect back what that need is, so that I'm sure everybody's communicating?" He couldn't do it. I had to repeat it two or three times before he could hear the other person's needs.

I reversed the process and said to the second chief, "I thank you for hearing that he has this need for security. Now I'd like to hear what your needs are in this." He said, "They have been trying to dominate us. They are a dominating group of people. They think they're better than everybody." Once again, this started a fight with the other side. I had to interrupt and say, "Excuse me, excuse me." After the group settled down, I went back to trying to sense the needs behind his statement that the other side was dominating.

I asked, "Chief, is your need behind that statement a need for equality? You really need to feel that you're being treated equally in this community?" And he said, "Yes, of course!"

Again, the job was to get the chief on the other side to hear, which wasn't easy. It took three or four repetitions before I could get the chief on the other side just to see the need that this other human being was expressing. Finally, the chief was able to hear the other chief saying he had a need for equality.

After I spent this much time getting both sides to express their needs and to hear each other's needs (this took close to two hours), another chief who hadn't spoken jumped to his feet, looked at me, and said something very intensely in his own language. I was very curious about what he was trying to express to me with such intensity, and I eagerly awaited the translation. I was very touched when the translator said, "The chief says we cannot learn this way of communicating in one day. But he says that if we know how to communicate this way, we don't have to kill each other."

I said to the translator, "Tell the chief I am very grateful that he sees what can happen when we hear each other's needs. Tell him that today my objective is to help resolve the conflict peacefully to everyone's satisfaction, and I am hoping that people can see the value in this way of communicating. Tell him that if people on both sides would like, we will be glad to train people within each tribe to communicate this way, so that future conflicts can be resolved this way rather than through violence."

That chief wanted to be one of the members to be trained. In fact, before I left that day, we had members from both tribes eager to learn this process that would allow everyone to hear needs behind whatever message was being expressed. I am happy to report that the war between the tribes ended that day.

Offering Strategies in Positive Action Language

After I help parties in a conflict express their needs and connect with the needs of others, I suggest we move on to look for strategies that meet everyone's needs. In my experience, if we move too quickly to strategies, we may find some compromises, but we won't have the same quality of resolution. However, if we thoroughly understand needs before moving to proposed solutions, we increase the likelihood that both parties will stay with the agreement.

Of course, it's not enough just to help each side see what the other side needs. We must end with action—action that meets everyone's needs. This requires that we be able to express proposed strategies clearly in present, positive action language.

By "present" language, I mean a clear statement of what is wanted from the other side *at this moment*. For example, start with, "I'd like you to tell me if you would be willing to . . . ," and then say the action that you would like the other person to take. Bringing it into the present by saying, "Would you be willing to . . . ?" makes it easier to foster a respectful discussion. If the other side says they are not willing, we can find out why. I've found that conflicts move more toward resolution if we can learn to say the request in present language.

If I say, "I'd like you to go to the show with me Saturday night," it's pretty clear what I want on Saturday night, but it doesn't necessarily make clear what I want from them at that moment. At that moment I may want them to tell me whether they would be willing to go. I may want them to tell me how they feel about going with me. I may want them to tell me whether they have any reservations about going, and so forth.

The more we can be clear about what response we're wanting *right now,* the more quickly conflict can move toward resolution.

I also suggest that requests be expressed in *positive action language* by stating clearly what we do want done to meet our needs, rather than what we don't want. In conflict situations, telling people what we don't want creates both confusion and resistance. This applies even when we're talking to ourselves. If we just tell ourselves what we don't want to do, we're not likely to make much change in the situation.

I can think of a time several years ago when I was debating an issue on public television. The program was recorded earlier in the day so it could be shown in the evening, and I was able to go home and watch it. While I was watching this program, I became very upset with myself, because I was doing three things I don't like doing when I'm debating. I remember saying to myself, "If I'm ever debating an issue like this again, I don't want to do A, I don't want to do B, I don't want to do C."

I had a chance to redeem myself, because the following week I was asked to continue the same debate. As I was going to the television station, I repeated to myself: "Now, remember, don't do A, don't do B, and don't do C." I got on the program, the other debater came at me the same way he had been communicating the previous week, and what did I do? For ten seconds I was beautiful. But what did I do after ten seconds? A, B, and C. In fact, as I recall, I quickly made up for the previous ten seconds!

The problem was that I had told myself what *not* to do. I hadn't been clear about exactly what I wanted to do differently. In conflict resolution, it helps both parties to say clearly what they do want—rather than what they don't want—in order to meet everyone's needs.

A woman made this point very clearly to me one time. She had a conflict with her husband about how much time he was spending at home, so she said to him, "I don't want you spending so much time at work." Afterward she got furious with him when he signed up for a bowling league. Here again, she had said what she didn't want, not what she did want. If she had expressed what she did want, it might have sounded like this, "I'd like you to tell me if you'd be willing to spend at least one evening a week with the children and me."

Action language means saying clearly what we do want when we make a request by using clear action verbs. It also means avoiding language that obscures our needs or that sounds like an attack.

For example, one couple had had a conflict for twelve years. The woman had a need for understanding that wasn't being met in the relationship. When I got her partner to reflect her need, I said, "Okay, now let's get down to strategies." I asked, "What do you want—from him, for example—to meet your need for understanding?" She looked at her husband and replied, "I'd like you to listen to me when I talk to you." He said, "I do listen." and she said, "No, you don't." And he said, "Yes, I do." They told me they'd had this same conversation for twelve years. This is what happens when we use words like *listen* to express our strategies. It's too vague. It's not an action verb.

With my help, this woman realized what she really wanted from her partner when she said, "I want you to listen." She wanted him to reflect back what she was saying, so that she could be sure she had made herself clear. When she made that positive action request of him, he was quite willing to do it. She was delighted because this strategy really met her need. Finally she was getting a need met that she had been very eager to have met for twelve years. All she had been lacking was clear language for telling him what she wanted.

A similar husband-and-wife conflict involved the wife's need for her husband to respect her choices. Once her husband understood, I said, "Now that your husband understands your need to have your choices respected, what are you requesting of him? What are your strategies for getting that need met?"

She said, "Well, I want you to give me the freedom to grow and be myself," and he replied, "I do." She responded, "No, you don't," and he said, "I do." Then I said, "Hold it! Hold on!"

Once again we see nonaction language exacerbating a conflict. People can easily hear "Give me the freedom to grow" as implying that they are a slave-master or domineering. This request doesn't make clear what *is* wanted. I pointed this out to the wife. I said, "I'd like you to tell him exactly what you want him to do to better meet your need for having your choices respected."

She replied, "I want you to allow me . . . ," and I stopped her and said, "I'm afraid that *allow* is vague also. Can you use a more concrete action verb than *allow?*"

She replied, "Well, how about if I want him to let me?" "No," I said. "That's still pretty vague. What do you really mean when you say you want a person to let you?"

After thinking it over for a few seconds, she came to an important awareness. She said, "Uh-oh, Marshall, I see what's going on. I know what I want from him when I say 'I want you to let me be' and 'I want you to give me the freedom to grow.' But if I say this in clear language, it's pretty embarrassing. Besides, I can see that he couldn't do it, because I want him to tell me it's okay no matter what I do."

When she got clear about what she was actually requesting, she saw that it didn't leave him much freedom to be himself and to have *his* choices respected. Respect is a key element of successful conflict resolution.

RESOLVING CONFLICTS WITH AUTHORITIES

I was working with a group of minority students in a Southern city many years ago. They had the impression that the principal of their school was very racist in many of his behaviors, and they wanted my help in developing skills to resolve their conflicts with him.

When we worked in our training session, they defined their needs clearly. When we talked about expressing their request, they said, "Marshall, we're not optimistic about making requests of him. We have made requests of him in the past, and it wasn't very pleasant. In the past, he has said, 'Get out of here, or I'm going to call the police.'" I asked, "What request did you make of him?"

One of the students replied, "We said we didn't want him telling us how we could wear our hair." They were referring to the fact that the principal barred them from the football team unless they cut their hair short. I pointed out to them, "Telling him what you don't want (you don't want him telling you how to wear your hair) is really not what I'm suggesting. I'm suggesting you learn how to tell him what you do want."

Another student said, "Well, we told him we wanted fairness." I responded, "Well, that's a need. We have a need for fairness. Once we know our needs, the next step is to be clear with people about what we really want them to do. What can they do to meet our needs? We have to learn how to say that more clearly."

We worked very hard and came up with thirty-eight requests in positive action language, and we practiced how to present the requests in a respectful, nondemanding way. Doing that means that after you make your request, no matter how the other person responds—whether the person says yes or no—you give an equal amount of respect and understanding. If they say no, try to understand *what need they are meeting* that keeps them from saying yes.

Respecting Is Not the Same as Conceding

Understanding other people's needs does not mean you have to give up your own needs. It does mean demonstrating to them that you are interested in *both* your needs *and* theirs. When they trust that, there's much more likelihood of everyone's needs getting met, which is what happened in the situation with the principal.

The students went in, told the principal their needs, and expressed their thirty-eight requests in clear action language. They listened to what needs the principal had, and in the end, the principal agreed to all thirty-eight of their requests. About two weeks later, I got a call from a representative of the school district asking if I would teach their school administrator what I had taught those students.

It's very important when expressing our requests to be respectful of the other person's reaction, regardless of whether that person agrees to the request. One of the most important messages another person can give us is "no" or "I don't want to." If we listen well to this message, it will help us understand the other person's needs. If we are listening to other people's needs, we will see that every time they say no, they're really saying they have a need that is not addressed by our strategy, which keeps them from saying yes. If we can teach ourselves to hear the need behind that no, we will find an openness toward getting everyone's needs met.

Of course, if we hear the no as a rejection, or if we start to blame the other person for saying no, then it's not likely that we're going to find a way of getting everyone's needs met. It's key that throughout the process we keep everyone's attention focused on *meeting everyone's needs.*

I'm very optimistic about what can happen in any conflict if we create this quality of connection. If all sides in a conflict get clear about what they need and hear the other side's needs and if people express their strategies in clear action language, then even if the other person says no, the focus returns to meeting *needs.* If we all do this, we will easily find strategies that get everyone's needs met.

WHEN YOU CAN'T GET THE TWO SIDES TOGETHER

As I said, I'm very optimistic about what can happen when we get people together and talking at this level, but that requires getting them together. In recent years, I have been looking for strategies for resolving conflicts in which we can't get both sides together.

One strategy that I'm very pleased with involves the use of a recorder. I work with each party separately and play the role of the other person. Here's what this looks like: A woman came to me very much in pain because of the conflict between her and her husband, especially because of how he was handling his anger and beating her at times. She wanted him to come to the meeting with her and talk about this conflict that they had, but he refused. When she came into my office, I said, "Let me play the role of your husband." In that role, I listened to what she was saying and respectfully heard the feelings that she was expressing and how it felt to her to be hit and to not be understood as she would like.

I listened in a way that helped her get her needs more clearly expressed and that showed a respectful understanding of her needs. Then, still in the role of the husband, I expressed what I guessed the husband's needs were and asked her to hear me. We recorded this role-play with me playing the role of the husband, and, with my help, we clearly communicated her needs. Then I asked her to take this recording to her husband and get his reaction to it.

When she took the recording to her husband and he heard how I had played his role, he felt a good deal of relief. Apparently, I had guessed accurately what his needs were. As a result of the understanding that he felt due to how I had empathically played his role, he did come in, and we continued to work together until they found other ways of meeting their needs besides violence.

CONCLUSION

I've been sharing some of my concepts of conflict resolution, showing how much I believe a literacy of needs helps, how important it is both to express needs and to hear the other side's needs, and then to look for strategies and to express them using clear action language.

I hope that what I've shared supports your efforts to resolve personal conflicts more harmoniously and that it also supports your efforts to mediate the conflicts of others. I hope it strengthens your awareness of the precious flow of communication that allows conflicts to be resolved so that everyone's needs are fulfilled. I also hope that it increases your awareness of the possibility of communication that precludes the necessity of coercion, a flow of communication that increases our awareness of our interdependence.

2

BEING ME, LOVING YOU

A Practical Guide to
Extraordinary Relationships

The following are excerpts from workshops and media interviews I've given on the subject of intimacy and close personal relationships. Through role-playing and discussion, I touch on most of the key aspects of applying Nonviolent Communication to create loving relationships with our partners, spouses, and family while maintaining our personal integrity and values.

WORKSHOP INTRODUCTION

So, guess what happened today? I'm doing this relationship workshop in the evening, and I had a crisis at seven o'clock this morning. My wife called and asked me one of those questions that you just hate to have in a relationship at any time of the day, but especially at seven in the morning when you don't have your lawyer. What did she ask at seven o'clock in the morning? "Did I wake you up?" That question wasn't the hard one. She says, "I have a very important question: Am I attractive?" [Laughter.] I hate those questions. That's like the time I came home after being on the road quite awhile, and she asked me, "Can you see anything different in the house?" I looked, and I looked: "No." She had painted the whole house! [Laughter.]

I knew that question this morning was the kind that comes up in relationships. "Am I attractive?" Of course, as an NVC-speaking person, I could get out of that by claiming that it's not an NVC question, because we know that nobody is anything. Nobody is right, wrong, attractive, or unattractive. But I knew she wouldn't settle for any of that stuff, so I said, "You want to know if you're attractive?" She said, "Yes." I said, "Sometimes yes, sometimes no; can I go back to bed?" [Laughter.] She liked that—thank goodness!

In one of my favorite books, *How to Make Yourself Miserable* by Dan Greenburg, you see this dialogue:

> *"Do you love me? Now, this is very important to me.*
> *Think it over: Do you love me?"*
> *"Yes."*
> *"Please, this is very important. Give it very serious consideration:*
> *Do you love me?"*
> *(Period of silence) "Yes."*
> *"Then why did you hesitate?" (Laughter.)*

People can change how they think and communicate. They can treat themselves with much more respect, and they can learn from their limitations without hating themselves. We teach people how to do this with Nonviolent Communication. We show people a process that can help them connect with the people they're closest to in a way that can allow them to enjoy deeper intimacy, to give to one another with more enjoyment, and to not get caught up in doing things out of duty, obligation, guilt, shame, and the other things that destroy intimate relationships. We show people how to enjoy working cooperatively in a working community. We show them how to transform domination structures and hierarchal structures into working communities in which people share a vision of how they can contribute to life. And we're thrilled with how many people all over the world have great energy for making this happen.

A TYPICAL CONFLICT

PARTICIPANT A: Marshall, what do you think is the major conflict, the major issue, between men and women?

MARSHALL: Well, I hear a lot of this in my work. Women come up to me regularly and say, "Marshall, I wouldn't want you to get the wrong idea. I have a very wonderful husband." And then, of course, I know the word *but* is coming. "But I never know how he's feeling." Men all over the planet (and there are exceptions to this) come from the John Wayne school of expressing emotions—the Clint Eastwood, the Rambo school—where you kind of grunt. Instead of saying clearly what's going on inside of you, you label people as John Wayne would when he walked into a tavern in the movies. He never, even if there were guns trained on him, said, "I'm scared." He might have been out in the desert for six months, but he never said, "I'm lonely." So how did John communicate? John communicated by labeling people. It's a simple classification system. They were either a good guy—buy them a drink—or a bad guy—kill them.

With that way of communicating, which was basically how I was trained to communicate, you don't learn how to get in touch with your own emotions. If you're being trained to be a warrior, you want to keep your feelings out of your consciousness. Well, to be married to a warrior is not a very rich experience for a woman who may have been playing dolls while the boys were out playing war. She wants intimacy, but the man doesn't have a vocabulary that makes it easy to do that.

On the other hand, women are not taught to be very clear about their needs. They've been taught for several centuries to deny their own needs and to take care of others. So they often depend on the man for leadership and expect him to kind of guess what they need and want and to fulfill that, to take care of that. I see these issues regularly, but, as I say, there are certainly a lot of individual differences.

PARTICIPANT A: Let's do a role-play, the kind of thing that happens between men and women. Can you set it up? I mean, what they fight about the most.

MARSHALL: Well, one of the most frequent issues is the woman saying to the man, "I don't feel the connection with you that I would like. I really want to feel more of an emotional connection with you. And how do you feel when I say that?" And the man says, "Huh?"

PARTICIPANT A: Well, yeah, let me play the man.

PARTICIPANT A, AS HUSBAND: Well, what do you want? What do you want me to do?

MARSHALL, AS WIFE: Well, like right now, instead of asking me that question, I would like to know what you're feeling. Are you hurt by what I said? Are you angry? Are you scared?

PARTICIPANT A, AS HUSBAND: I don't know.

MARSHALL, AS WIFE: This is what I mean. When you don't know what you're feeling, it's very hard for me to feel safe and trusting.

PARTICIPANT A, AS HUSBAND: Well, I feel like you're . . . I feel like you're criticizing me.

MARSHALL, AS WIFE: So you're feeling kind of hurt, and you want me to respect you and to appreciate what you offer in our relationship.

PARTICIPANT A, AS HUSBAND: Well, yeah.

MARSHALL, AS WIFE: And see, I would've liked for you to have said that. I would've liked to have heard you say, "I'm hurt, I'd like some appreciation." But notice you didn't say that. You said, "You're criticizing me." You required me to have to take a deep breath and not get caught up in that and not hear a judgment in what you say, and instead to try to hear what you're feeling and what you might need. I'd like not to work so hard at that. I'd really appreciate it if you could just tell me what's going on inside you.

PARTICIPANT A, AS HUSBAND: Well, I don't know what's going on inside of me most of the time. What do you want from me?

MARSHALL, AS WIFE: Well, first, I am just glad we're having this conversation now. I want you to know that I hope I can stay aware of how confusing it is for you to give me what I want. I'm trying to become conscious that it is such a new thing for you, and I want to be patient. But I would like to hear what's going on in you.

PARTICIPANT A, AS HUSBAND: Well, right now, I guess I'm just glad that you're telling me what you need.

MARSHALL, AS HIMSELF: That's a very typical kind of interaction that goes on. The man very often hears demands coming from the woman.

ON THE SUBJECT OF MARRIAGE

You may have heard me say that it is harder to relate within a marriage than outside because of all the crazy things we are taught about what "marriage" means. I find I enjoy the person I'm living with much more if I don't think of her as "my wife," because in the culture I grew up in, when men say "my wife" they start to think of her as some kind of property.

NVC is a language that makes it possible for us to connect with one another in a way that enables us to give to each other from the heart. This means that with your partner you don't do things because of titles that imply you are "supposed to," "should," "ought to," or "must." You don't give out of guilt, shame, unconsciousness, fear, obligation, or duty. It is my belief that whenever we do anything for one another out of that kind of energy, everybody loses. When we receive something given out of that kind of energy, we know we are going to have to pay for it, because it was done at the other person's expense. I'm interested in a process in which we give to each other from the heart.

How do we learn to give from the heart in such a way that giving feels like receiving? When things are being done in a human way, I don't think you can tell the giver from the receiver. It's only when we interact in what I call a judging or judgmental manner that giving isn't much fun.

LEARNING THROUGH FOUR QUESTIONS

Let me suggest that you write some things down. I'm going to ask you four questions. If you are married or partnered, then pretend that I am asking you as your partner or spouse. If you want to focus on some other relationship, pick someone you're close to—perhaps a good friend.

As your NVC partner, I'm going to ask you the four questions that deeply interest NVC-speaking people about all relationships, but particularly intimate ones. Please write down your answer to each of these four questions as though you were asked by this other person. [Reader: I invite you to do this on your own on a separate sheet of paper.]

The first question: *Would you tell me one thing that I do as your partner or friend that makes life less than wonderful for you?* As an NVCer, I don't want to take any action or say anything that doesn't enrich your life. So it would be a great service if any time I do something that isn't enriching your life, you bring that to my attention. Could you think of one thing that I do—or don't do—that makes life less than wonderful for you? Write down one thing.

Now, the second question. As an NVC-speaking person, not only do I want to know what I do that makes life less than wonderful for you, but it's also important for me to be able to connect with your feelings moment by moment. To be able to play the game of giving to one another from our hearts, your feelings are critical and I need to be aware of them. It's stimulating when we can be in touch with one another's feelings. My second question then is, *When I do what I do, how do you feel?*

Write down how you feel.

Let's move to the third question. As an NVC-speaking person, I realize that how we feel is a result of what our needs are and what is happening to our needs. When our needs are getting fulfilled, we have feelings that fall under the heading of "pleasurable feelings," like happy, satisfied, joyful, blissful, and content. When our needs are not being satisfied, we have the kind of feelings that you just wrote down. So, this is question three: *What needs of yours are not getting met?*

I'd like you to tell me why you feel as you do in terms of your needs: "I feel as I do because I would have liked _____" (or "because I was wanting, wishing, or hoping for _____"). Write down your unmet needs in this format.

Now the NVCer is excited, because he wants to get on to the next question, which is the center of life for all NVC-speaking people. I can't wait to hear the answer to this. Is everybody ready for the big NVC question?

I am aware that I am doing something that is not enriching your life and that you have certain feelings about that. You've told me what needs of yours are not getting fulfilled. Now, please tell me what I can do to make your most wonderful dreams come true. That is what NVC is all about: *What can we do to enrich one another's lives?*

NVC is about clearly communicating those four things to other people at any given moment. Of course, the situation is not always about our needs getting met. We also say thank you in NVC and tell people how they have truly enriched our lives by telling them the first three things. We tell them (1) what they've done to enrich us, (2) what our feelings are, and (3) what needs of ours have been fulfilled by their actions. I believe that, as human beings, there are only two things that we are basically saying: please and thank you. The language of NVC is set up to make our please and thank you very clear so that people do not hear anything that gets in the way of our giving to one another from the heart.

Criticism

There are primarily two forms of communication that make giving from the heart almost impossible for people. The first is anything that sounds to them like a criticism. If you expressed your four answers in NVC, then there should be no words written there that can be heard by others as a criticism of them. As you can see, the only time you are talking about them is in the first part, where you mention their behavior. You are not criticizing them for the behavior; you are just calling that behavior to their attention. The other three parts are all about you: your feelings, your unmet needs, and your requests. If you use any words that can easily be heard by others as criticism, then my guess is that you've mixed a bit of judgment into those four ingredients.

By *criticism*, I mean attack, judgment, blame, diagnosis, or anything that analyzes people from the head. If your answers are in NVC, there will hopefully be no words that are easy to pick up as criticism. However, if the other person is wearing judging ears [Marshall puts on a pair of judging ears], they can hear criticism no matter what you say. Tonight we'll learn how to clean up such a mess if it happens. We want to be able to speak NVC to anybody.

Coercion

The second block to our ability to give from the heart is any hint of coercion. As an NVCer, you want to be able to present those four things you wrote down so that the other person receives them as a gift, an opportunity to give, not as a demand or an order. There is no criticism or coercion in NVC language. When we tell others what we want, we do so in a way that communicates to them, "Please, do this only if you can do so willingly. Please, never do anything for me at your expense. Never do anything for me if there is the least bit of fear, guilt, shame, resentment, or resignation behind your motives. Otherwise we'll both suffer. Please, honor my request only if it comes from your heart, where it is a gift to yourself to give to me." Only when neither person feels like they're losing, giving in, or giving up do both people benefit from the action.

Receiving from the Heart

There are two main parts to NVC: The first is the ability to say those four things and get them across to the other person without the other person hearing criticism or demand. The other part is to learn how to receive these four pieces of information from others, regardless of whether they speak a judging language or NVC. If the other person speaks NVC, our life will be a lot easier. That person will say these four things with clarity, and our job will be to accurately receive them before we react.

However, if the other person speaks a judging language, then we need to put on "NVC ears." [Laughter as Marshall dons a set of NVC ears.] NVC ears serve as a translator: no matter what language the other person speaks, when we have these ears on, we only hear NVC. For example, the other person says, "The problem with you is _____;" but with NVC ears, I hear, "What I would like is _____." I hear no judgment, criticism, or attack. With these ears on, I realize that all criticism is a pathetic expression of an unmet need—pathetic because it usually doesn't get the person what they want and instead causes all kinds of tension and problems. With NVC, we skip through all that. We never hear a criticism, just unmet needs.

Listening and Responding in NVC

Let's practice listening in NVC when people speak judgmentally. I would like some people to volunteer their situations so we can all learn from them. If you read what you wrote, we'll see if you answered in NVC or whether some judging language got mixed in.

The first question: "What is it that I do that makes life less than wonderful for you?"

PARTICIPANT B: You appear not to listen.

MARSHALL: "You appear." Right away I can tell you aren't answering the question in NVC. When you say "you appear," I know a diagnosis is coming up. "You appear not to listen"—that's a diagnosis. Have you ever heard one person say, "You don't listen," and the other, "I do, too!" "No, you don't!" "Yes, I do!" You see? This is what happens when we start with a criticism rather than an observation.

MARSHALL, AS PARTNER: Tell me what I do that makes you interpret me as not listening. I can read the newspaper and watch television while you're talking and still hear you.

PARTICIPANT B: I'm observing you watching TV.

MARSHALL, AS HIMSELF: If your partner weren't listening with NVC, right away he'd hear an attack. But as your partner with NVC ears, I don't hear criticism; I just guess the behavior you are reacting to.

MARSHALL, AS PARTNER: Are you reacting to the fact that I am watching television while you are talking to me?

PARTICIPANT B: Yes.

MARSHALL, AS PARTNER: How do you feel when I watch television while you are talking?

MARSHALL, AS HIMSELF: [In an aside to the participant.] And don't answer, "I feel not listened to!" That's just a sneaky way of throwing in another judgment.

PARTICIPANT B: I feel frustrated and hurt.

MARSHALL, AS HIMSELF: Now we're cooking!

MARSHALL, AS PARTNER: Could you tell me why you feel that way?

PARTICIPANT B: Because I want to feel appreciated.

MARSHALL, AS HIMSELF: Classic NVC! Notice she didn't say, "I feel frustrated and hurt because you watch television." She doesn't blame me for her feelings, but she attributes them to her own needs: "I feel _____ because I _____." People who judge, on the other hand, would express their feelings this way: "You hurt me when you watch television while talking to me." In other words: "I feel _____ because you _____."

Now the fourth question: "What would you like me to do to make life wonderful for you?"

PARTICIPANT B: When you are in a conversation, I would appreciate it if you would look into my eyes, as well as tell me back what you heard me say. •

MARSHALL: Okay. Did everybody hear the four things? "When you watch television while I am talking, I feel frustrated and hurt because I would really like some appreciation or attention regarding what I am saying. Would you be willing to look me in the eye while I'm talking and then afterward repeat back what you heard me say and give me a chance to correct it if it isn't what I meant to say?"

Now of course, the other person may hear it as criticism and will want to defend himself: "I do listen; I can listen while I am watching television." Or if he heard it as a demand, he may do this: "[Sigh.] All right." That tells us he didn't hear it as a request, as an opportunity to contribute to our well-being. He heard a demand; he may comply, but if he does, you'll wish he hadn't because he'll be doing it to keep you from freaking out. He'll do it not to make life wonderful for you but to keep life from being miserable for him.

That's why marriage is a real challenge. Many people were taught that love and marriage mean denying oneself in doing for the other person. "If I love her, I have to do that, even though I don't want to." So he'll do it, but you'll wish he hadn't.

PARTICIPANT B: Because he'll keep score.

MARSHALL: Yeah, people like that have computers in their brains: they'll tell you what happened twelve years ago when they denied themselves. It comes back in one form or another. "After all the times I did things for you when I didn't want to, the least you can do is _____!" Oh yeah, that goes on forever; don't worry, they're excellent statisticians.

ROLE-PLAYS

Hearing a Demand

PARTICIPANT C: So how does the NVCer respond when the person says, "I can listen to you and watch at the same time"?

MARSHALL, AS NVCER: Are you feeling annoyed because you heard some pressure, and you would like to be free from pressure?

PARTICIPANT C: Of course! You're always making demands. My God! Demand this, demand that!

MARSHALL, AS NVCER: So you're kind of exhausted with demands, and you would like to do things because you feel like it and not because you feel pressured?

PARTICIPANT C: Exactly.

MARSHALL, AS NVCER: Now I'm feeling very frustrated because I don't know how to let you know what I would like without you hearing it as a demand. I know only two choices: to say nothing and not get my needs met, or to tell you what I would like and have you hear it as a demand. Either way, I lose. Could you tell me what you just heard me say?

PARTICIPANT C: Huh?

MARSHALL, AS HIMSELF: Now, this is very confusing for people who don't know NVC. They grow up in a world of coercion. Their parents might have thought that the only way to get them to do anything was to punish or guilt-trip them. They may not be familiar with anything else. They don't know the difference between a request and a demand. They really believe that if they don't do what the other person wants, the guilt trip or the threats are going to come out. It is not an easy job for me as an NVCer to help this person hear that my requests are gifts, not demands. When we do succeed, however, we can save ourselves years of misery, because any request becomes misery when people hear it without NVC ears.

MARSHALL, AS NVCER: I would like to know how I can ask for what I want so it doesn't sound like I am pressuring you.

PARTICIPANT C: I don't know.

MARSHALL, AS NVCER: Well, I'm glad that we're getting this clear, because this is my dilemma: I don't know how to let you know what I want without you immediately hearing either that you have to do it or that I am forcing you to do it.

PARTICIPANT C: Well, I know how much the thing means to you, and . . . if you love somebody, then you do what they ask.

MARSHALL, AS NVCER: Could I influence you to change your definition of love?

PARTICIPANT C: To what?

MARSHALL, AS NVCER: Love is not denying ourselves and doing for others; rather, it is honestly expressing whatever our feelings and needs are and empathically receiving the other person's feelings and needs. To receive empathically does not mean that you must comply—just accurately receive what is expressed as a gift of life from the other person. Love is honestly expressing our own needs; that doesn't mean making demands, but just, "Here I am. Here's what I like." How do you feel about that definition of love?

PARTICIPANT C: If I agree with that, I'll be a different person.

MARSHALL, AS NVCER: Yeah, that's true. •

Stop Me If I'm Talking "Too Much"

MARSHALL: How about another situation?

PARTICIPANT D: Sometimes people say, "I want you to be quiet; I don't want to listen any more," if they are feeling overwhelmed. In a situation where the other person is talking too much . . .

MARSHALL: If you're an NVCer, you don't have the words "too much" in your consciousness. To think that there is such a thing as "too much," "just right," or "too little" is to entertain dangerous concepts.

PARTICIPANT D: What I heard you and the other trainers telling me last night is that I have to stop once in a while to give the other person a chance to respond.

MARSHALL: "Have to?"

PARTICIPANT D: No, not "have to." I mean "it would be a good idea to."

MARSHALL: Yes, you know you don't have to, because there have been a lot of times in your life when you haven't. [Laughter.]

PARTICIPANT D: Well, I'd like to get some sort of signal from my friend . . .

MARSHALL: When he's heard one more word than he wants to hear?

PARTICIPANT D: Right.

MARSHALL: The kindest thing we can do is stop people when they are using more words than we want to hear. Notice the difference: It's not "when they are talking much." I say "kindest" because I have asked several hundred people, "If you are using more words than somebody wants to hear, do you want that other person to pretend that they are listening or to stop you?" Everyone but one person replied adamantly, "I want to be stopped." Only one woman said she didn't know if she could handle being told to stop.

In NVC, we know it's not being kind to the other person to smile and open your eyes wide to hide the fact that your head has gone dead. That isn't helping anybody, because the person in front of you becomes a source of stress and strain, and nobody wants that. People want every act and every word coming out of their mouths to enrich you. So when that isn't happening, be kind to them and stop them.

Now it took me awhile to get up the courage to test this out, because in the domination culture I grew up in, that's not done. I remember when I first decided to risk this in a social setting. I was working with some teachers in Fargo, North Dakota, and I was invited to a social get-together, with everybody sitting around talking about stuff. Within ten minutes, my energy had dropped very low. I didn't know where the life was in this conversation or what people were feeling or wanting. One person would say, "Oh, do you know what we did on our vacation?" and then they would talk about the vacation. Then somebody else talked about theirs.

After listening awhile, I gathered up my courage and said, "Excuse me, I'm impatient with the conversation because I'm really not feeling as connected with you as I'd like to be. It would help me to know if you are enjoying the conversation." If they were, I would try to figure out how to enjoy it myself; but all nine people stopped talking and looked at me as if I had thrown a rat in the punch bowl.

For about two minutes I thought I'd die, but then I remembered that it's never the response I receive that makes me feel bad. Since I was feeling bad, I knew I had on my judging ears and was thinking that I had said something wrong. After I put on my NVC ears, I was able to look at the feelings and needs being expressed through the silence and say, "I'm guessing that you're all angry with me, and you would have liked for me to have just kept out of the conversation."

The moment I turn my attention to what the other is feeling and needing, already I am feeling better. With my attention there, I totally remove the other person's power to demoralize or dehumanize me or to leave me feeling like PPPPPT (piss poor protoplasm poorly put together). This is true even when, as in this case, I guess wrong. Just because I have NVC ears doesn't mean I always guess right. I guessed they were angry, and they weren't.

The first person who spoke told me, "No, I'm not angry. I was just thinking about what you were saying." Then he said, "I *was* bored with this conversation." And he had been the one doing most of the talking! But this no longer surprises me; I have found that if I am bored, the person doing the talking is probably equally bored. It usually means we are not talking from life; instead of being in touch with our feelings and needs in this conversation, we're getting into some socially learned habits of boring one another. If you are a middle-class citizen, you are probably so used to it that you don't even know it.

I remember Buddy Hackett saying it wasn't until he was in the army that he discovered he could get up from a meal without having heartburn. He had been so used to his mother's cooking that heartburn had become a way of life. Likewise, most middle-class people are so used to boredom that it's become a way of life. You just get together and talk from the head; there is no life in it, but it's the only thing you've known. We're dead and don't know it.

When we went around our group, each one of the nine people expressed the same feelings I had been feeling: impatient, discouraged that we were there, lifeless, inert. Then one of the women asked, "Marshall, why do we do this?" "Do what?" "Sit around and bore each other. You're just here tonight, but we get together every week and do this!" I said, "Because we probably haven't learned to take the risk that I just did, which is to pay attention to our vitality. Are we really getting what we want from life? If not, let's do something about it. Each moment is precious, too precious. So when our vitality is down, let's do something about it and wake up."

"What Do You Want from Me?"

PARTICIPANT E: Marshall, I was thinking about how sometimes we women get together with our men, and we drive around and say, "Oh, isn't that a cute house?" or "Look at that lake—that's the one I want to go on." They think they have to get us a new house or take us to the lake right away, but even though we may seem enthusiastic, we're not asking for anything—we're just talking out loud.

MARSHALL: Now, I want to defend men—and not just men. When you say something and don't say what you want back from others, you create more pain in relationships than you are probably conscious of. Other people have to guess, "Does she want me to say something cute and superficial about this thing, or is she really trying to tell me something else?"

It's like the gentleman sitting next to his wife on the little train at the Dallas airport that connects the terminals. I was sitting across from them. This train was going very slowly, and the man turned to his wife in a great state of agitation and said, "I have never seen a train go so slowly in all of my life." Notice how that is similar to "Isn't that an interesting house?" What did she want there? What does he want here? He wasn't aware of the amount of pain it creates for the other person when we just give commentary and don't make explicit what we want back. It's a guessing game. But knowing what you want back from your words requires a consciousness of living in the moment, of being fully present right now. So he didn't say anything more than, "I've never seen a train go so slowly in my whole life."

Sitting right across from them, I could see that she was uncomfortable: somebody she loves is in pain, and she doesn't know what he wants. So she did what most of us do when we don't know what a person is wanting from us: she said nothing.

Then he did what most of us do when we're not getting what we want: he repeated himself, as though magically if you just keep repeating yourself you'll get what you want. We don't realize that just burns other people's brains out.

So again he said, "I have never seen a train go so slowly in all of my life!"

I loved her response: she said, "They're electronically timed." I don't think that's what he wanted. Why would she give him information that he already knows? Because she was trying to be a fixer, trying to make it better. She didn't know what to do, and he had contributed to her pain by not telling her what he wanted.

So he repeated himself a third time, "I have never seen a train go so slowly in all of my life!" And then she said, "Well, what do you want me to do about it?"

You see, what he wanted is what each of us wants every day, and when we don't get it, there is a significant effect on our morale. We want it every day, usually more than one time a day, and when we don't get it, we pay a high cost. Most of the time when we want it, we're not conscious of it, and even if we are conscious of it, we don't know how to ask for it. It's tragic.

I am confident that what he wanted was empathy. He wanted a response that would tell him that she was in contact with his feelings and needs.

If they had studied NVC, the conversation might have sounded like this:

HUSBAND: Boy, I've never seen a train go so slowly in all of my life! Could you just reflect back right now what I'm feeling and needing?

WIFE: So I guess you're really aggravated, and you wish they would have managed these trains differently.

HUSBAND: Yes, and more than that, you know if we don't get there in time, then we're going to be late, and we might have to pay extra for our tickets.

WIFE: So you're scared, and you'd like to get there on time so that we don't have to end up paying more money.

HUSBAND: Yeah [sigh].

When we are in pain, there is something enormously valuable to just having another person in contact with it. It's amazing how that kind of attention can make such a difference. It doesn't solve our problem, but it provides the kind of connection that lets the problem-solving become more bearable. When we don't get that—as he didn't—then we both end up in more pain than when we started.

Issues about Food

PARTICIPANT F: Marshall, can I share something that happened last night? I felt bad that my husband couldn't be there for the second night of the partner workshop. I got home at 11 p.m., and he called at about 11:05 from his motel. I related what had happened in the class and what he had missed—the group had discussed eating issues, which were important to me because I'm a compulsive eater. My husband and I had gotten to the point where he didn't even want to discuss food with me, because he thought I was killing myself with food. It was so painful for him, he wouldn't even talk about it.

So I told him about your suggestion and what had gone on at the workshop, and he opened up for the first time in years. When he gets home from teaching, he eats an ice cream to deal with emotions that come from a bad teaching day, and so we were able to actually give each other a lot of empathy over eating as a way to hide from the pain.

Then yesterday I got in contact—really in contact. I wanted some Almond Mocha candy, so I just imagined the chocolate and the almonds and the crunchy stuff underneath. And I thought, "What am I really looking for?" Love! It was just like a flashbulb going off in my head: what I am looking for is love.

MARSHALL: You wanted some kind of connection with him. And in the past, not knowing how to ask for that connection, it might have taken the form of candy.

PARTICIPANT F: Yes, it was great! We talked for an hour long distance. I think it was a first opening.

MARSHALL: So two nights in a row you've had a real connection! Now we have to get you talking NVC with yourself and away from thinking that there really is such a thing as a "compulsive overeater." You can't say those words in NVC, because there are no judgments in NVC. Remember, all judgments are tragic expressions of other things. NVC is a process. When we say anything about ourselves like, "I am a _____," it's static thinking; it puts us in a box and leads to self-fulfilling prophecies. When we think that we (or somebody else) *is* something, we usually act in a way that makes it happen. There is no verb "to be" in NVC; you can't say, "This person is lazy," "This person is normal," "This person is right." Let's translate "compulsive overeater" into NVC. Use the four things you have already worked with tonight.

PARTICIPANT F: "Whenever I eat out of my needs to be loved or to be touched . . ."

MARSHALL: I feel how?

PARTICIPANT F: "I feel that the food is assuaging me in a way that . . ."

MARSHALL: "I feel discouraged . . .?"

PARTICIPANT F: "I feel discouraged that I am not getting my needs met."

MARSHALL: "I feel discouraged because I really want to get clear on what my needs are so I can meet them."

PARTICIPANT F: Yes, right.

MARSHALL: "So I want to continue doing what I did last night with Bill on the phone. Now when I feel this urge, I want to stop and ask myself, 'What do I really need?'" You see how we have translated the judgment, "I'm a compulsive overeater" into how I feel, what my unmet needs are, and what I want to do about it. That's how we speak NVC with ourselves.

"When I eat because I want something else . . ." That's the first part, the observation of what she sees herself doing. Second, she checks her feeling: "I feel discouraged." Number three: "My unmet need is to be in touch with what I really want so I have a chance of getting it." And finally the fourth thing is, "What do I want to do about this to make my most wonderful dream come true? When I start finding myself wanting to eat, I stop and ask myself, 'What is it that I really need?' Then I get in touch with what I really need."

Now she is not thinking of what she is; she's more in touch with a process that moves. That may not solve the problem, but she'll find out by doing it, because she isn't thinking of what she is. She is thinking of what she is feeling and wanting and what she is going to do about that. As an NVCer, never think of yourself as a "worthwhile person." If you do, you will spend a good amount of time questioning whether you are a "worthless person." NVCers don't spend time thinking about what kind of person they are; they think moment by moment—not "What am I?" but "What is the life that is going on in me at this moment?"

Figuring Out What We Want

PARTICIPANT G: Sometimes we get into doing everything ourselves, and we are not in touch with how good it may feel to have someone else do for us. While you were talking to Participant F, I thought how nice it was to be in touch with what one needed. Sometimes I just don't know what I need, and I get discouraged.

MARSHALL: Most of us don't know what we want. It's only after we get something and it messes up our life that we know it wasn't what we wanted. I'll say I want an ice cream cone, get one, eat it, then feel terrible and realize that wasn't what I wanted.

To an NVCer, it's not a matter of knowing what is right or wrong. To use the language of life requires courage and choosing what you want based more on intuition than on thinking. It's being in touch with your unmet needs and choosing what you want to do about them.

PARTICIPANT G: I find that I'm a big doer.

MARSHALL: You just labeled yourself.

PARTICIPANT G: What I mean is that I run around wanting to connect with people by doing something for them. Sometimes I run across people who don't expect that from me, and it feels so good. But then

I start to wonder whether they would really like to receive but just won't let me in.

When Others Won't Receive

MARSHALL: That's probably because all their lives they have had people doing things for them and then sending them a bill. It's scary, so now they don't trust you either. They don't realize there is another kind of giving, that there are people who give not to take care of them but who give from the heart.

PARTICIPANT G: I'm sad that I haven't been able to clearly communicate that what I want is to give from the heart. Perhaps I can say to them, "It makes me sad that you don't give me the opportunity to give of myself."

MARSHALL: If you stop there, then we're back to the man on the train.

PARTICIPANT G: How about if I add, "Are you willing to tell me if you are willing to give me that opportunity?"

MARSHALL: Okay, I'm glad that you got that part in. You feel sad because you would really like the opportunity to give to them, to have them receive and feel comfortable with your gift.

PARTICIPANT G: Right, it's really simple.

Are We Arguing?

PARTICIPANT H: I feel frustrated when I try to talk with my girlfriend, because she tells me she doesn't want to argue. Any time I try to express my feelings and needs, she thinks I'm arguing. She says she doesn't want to argue in front of her kid (who is there all the time).

MARSHALL: Oh, yes, that's a rough one. If people see us as trying to argue, then they think that we are trying to win. It's hard to convince them otherwise, because people with a judgmental mentality have little idea how you can express feelings and wants without somebody being wrong.

PARTICIPANT H: But the hard part is she thinks I am arguing even if I try to empathize with her. When I try to guess her feelings and wants, she sees it as "arguing."

MARSHALL: Because she doesn't want you to judge her. She's afraid once she acknowledges what you say or allows herself to become vulnerable, you are going to zap her and tell her she's wrong for having those feelings and wants.

PARTICIPANT H: Well, according to her, the reason that she really doesn't like to deal with this kind of stuff is because she just wants the nice parts of life, not all that other heavy stuff.

MARSHALL: Yes, life is so full of unpleasant stuff as it is, so why deal with anything unpleasant?

PARTICIPANT H: Yes, right.

MARSHALL: That's exactly what my dad said at the first workshop that he came to. It's a lovable message, if you look at it that way. But when he first got clear from everybody in the group what a gift it would be to feel pain from their father if their father could just express it—to think of his feelings and needs as a gift—it was a mind-boggler for him. Since that time, there have been a lot of radical changes in him.

Certainly many people think that to talk about painful feelings is a negative, unpleasant experience, because they associate it with guilt games, punishment, and all kinds of other stuff. They haven't seen it as part of an NVC dance and how beautiful it can be to talk about those feelings. When I wrote the first edition of my book, I put in a list of positive feelings and a list of negative feelings. Then I noticed how people think negative feelings are negative. Since that's not what I wanted, in my next edition I put the words "positive" and "negative" in quotes, but that still didn't seem to help. Now I write, "feelings present when our needs are being meet" and "feelings present when our needs are not being met" to show how valuable they both are, because they are both talking about life.

So we have some work to do to convince your friend about this.

MARSHALL, AS GIRLFRIEND: Look, I don't want to argue. There is enough unpleasantness. Why can't we have a pleasant evening and watch television and enjoy one another?

PARTICIPANT H, AS NVCER: So you're feeling irritated . . .

MARSHALL, AS GIRLFRIEND: There you go again! Always talking about feelings!

PARTICIPANT H, AS HIMSELF: [Silence.] Uh-oh.

MARSHALL, AS HIMSELF: [Addressing laughter in the audience.] So you like seeing this rascal suffer?!

MARSHALL, AS GIRLFRIEND: I can't stand it when you do this! [Then she goes into the other room and slams the door.]

PARTICIPANT H, AS HIMSELF: It's more likely she would throw a lot of words at me, and I would just get knocked down for the count. [Laughter.]

MARSHALL: The ten count! Okay, so you play her and come on with those words.

MARSHÁLL, AS NVCER: So you really want to talk . . .

PARTICIPANT H, AS GIRLFRIEND: Stop! Stop! Don't bring this stuff up to me, because I don't like it.

MARSHALL, AS NVCER: I'm feeling very discouraged because I . . .

PARTICIPANT H, AS GIRLFRIEND: Why can't you just be the nice guy, the one I enjoy having a good time with? Let's be loving and forget about this stuff!

MARSHALL, AS NVCER: So you would like our evening to be light and easy, just enjoying one another?

PARTICIPANT H, AS GIRLFRIEND: Yeah.

MARSHALL, AS NVCER: I like that part of our relationship too, and I find that comes when we can deal with everything. You see, I want to laugh all my laughter and cry all my tears, and if I cut off half of it, then I find that the other half goes too. That's important. Can you tell me what you heard?

PARTICIPANT H, AS GIRLFRIEND: You are starting in again about feelings and getting depressed. I don't want to hear about it!

MARSHALL, AS NVCER: So, you're really afraid of getting down into those depressed feelings and want to stay out of them?

PARTICIPANT H, AS GIRLFRIEND: Yeah, and besides, tonight, with my kid around, I don't want us to argue.

MARSHALL, AS NVCER: Are you afraid that we are going to fight?

PARTICIPANT H, AS GIRLFRIEND: Please stop!

MARSHALL, AS NVCER: How would you feel about our continuing this when he is not here?

PARTICIPANT H, AS GIRLFRIEND: Yeah, you can come and meet me for lunch if you want to.

[At lunch.]

MARSHALL, AS NVCER: I'd like to show you a way that feelings could be very positive, regardless of which feelings they are.

PARTICIPANT H, AS GIRLFRIEND: I don't want to hear that stuff. Have you been taking those workshops again? [Laughter.] I want to concentrate on the positive things of life. I don't want to bring up hard feelings. I just want to enjoy the good stuff.

MARSHALL, AS NVCER: You really want to enjoy life and not get stuck down in some hole talking about negative stuff?

PARTICIPANT H, AS GIRLFRIEND: Yeah, I don't want that stuff in my life. Do you know what happened to Emily today? She went to pick up her boy and couldn't find him anywhere. At first she thought he'd gone home with their neighbor. But then she ran into one of the kids, and he told her that he saw her son leaving school at lunchtime with a man, a guy he'd never seen. Well, you can imagine how Emily was, especially after that thing that happened to her sister's kid two years ago. Remember? I think I told you about the time her sister was visiting and—

MARSHALL, AS NVCER: Excuse me for interrupting. Are you saying that it's a scary experience to hear things like that happening?

MARSHALL, AS HIMSELF: Do you see what I did? The girlfriend was using more words than I wanted to hear, and my energy started to drop. So I interrupted NVC style to connect with the feelings behind her words in that moment. I am not trying to take the floor away from the other person but to bring life back into the conversation. As I mentioned, my guess is that if I'm bored, so is the other person, so this would be a service to them as well as to me.

MARSHALL, AS NVCER: You are telling me that it was a real scary experience for you?

PARTICIPANT H, AS GIRLFRIEND: Yeah, he might run into the street and—

MARSHALL, AS NVCER: It really scares you to see just how close we all are to getting the life taken out of us at every moment.

PARTICIPANT H, AS GIRLFRIEND: Don't start that stuff on me again. He was just out in the street, and then his mom came after him again—

MARSHALL, AS NVCER: Excuse me, excuse me for interrupting. I'm feeling really impatient, because I'm not getting the connection in our conversations that I would like.

PARTICIPANT H, AS GIRLFRIEND: Okay, but I have to go anyway. I've got to go and pick up my kid now. School is going to be out—

MARSHALL, AS NVCER: I'd like you to tell me whether you have any interest in continuing our relationship.

PARTICIPANT H, AS GIRLFRIEND: Sure, you know that I really love you and want to be with you.

MARSHALL, AS NVCER: I really don't know how to continue our relationship, because there are certain things that I need in a relationship that I'm not getting, such as the ability to talk about certain feelings. If that is different from what you want in a relationship, then I would just like to get that clear so that we can have an NVC breakup.

PARTICIPANT H, AS GIRLFRIEND: [Suddenly speaking NVC.] So you're really feeling frustrated because you want to express your feelings and needs?

MARSHALL, AS NVCER: That's what I want, but I don't know how you need to be in a personal relationship.

MARSHALL, AS HIMSELF: There are people who want to keep things at that level, and they have a right to find somebody who wants to stay there with them. But I have never found anybody who really did. Often they have the erroneous idea that I want them to be associating with things in the past that are painful. Usually I am able to show them the difference between what they think I am talking about and what I am really talking about. With this particular girlfriend, I might have to be very clever to get that in, because she wasn't giving me much space.

Hearing No

PARTICIPANT I: I know that NVC is about figuring out my needs and requesting what I want, but that doesn't work with my boyfriend. If I start asking him for what I want, he'll just get really angry and huffy. Then I'll tell him to act decently, or maybe I'll wish I hadn't mentioned any of it in the first place.

MARSHALL: It's amazing how it just turns people into beasts when they hear that word. They beast themselves, and they beast the speaker, and it's a very small word—only two letters. Can anybody guess what the word is?

LOTS OF PARTICIPANTS: *No!*

MARSHALL: Yeah. It's amazing how people are so frightened of this word that they are afraid to ask for what they want, because what if the other person says no? I tell them it's not the *no* that bothers them, and they say, "Yes, it is; I'm so afraid of it." The problem is never the *no*; it's what we tell ourselves when the person says no. If we tell ourselves that it is a rejection, that's a problem, because it hurts. Rejection, ugh. Of course, if we have NVC ears on we would never hear *no*. We would be aware that a *no* is just a sloppy expression of what a person wants. We don't hear the slop; we just hear the want. It takes some practice.

MARSHALL, ADDRESSING PARTICIPANT I: So how did this boyfriend say no to you?

PARTICIPANT I: Well, I asked for something, and he said, *"No!"* And so I said—

MARSHALL: With that kind of energy already, we know what the problem is. He heard what, folks?

PARTICIPANTS: Demand.

MARSHALL: He heard a demand. Whenever people say no like that, they're scared to death that their autonomy is going to be taken away. They're afraid that if they really hear what the other person wants, they're going to get sucked in and have to do it, whether they want to or not. So when people say no like that, we know they didn't hear our request. It has nothing to do with us; it's obviously not a rejection, because they didn't even hear the request—they heard demand.

PARTICIPANT I: So at this point, I tried guessing what he was feeling, and he said, "I just want you to understand, to get it. I don't want to play this game, and I don't have to. I just want you to get the fact that the answer is no."

MARSHALL, AS BOYFRIEND: Just realize how scared I am about having my autonomy taken away.

MARSHALL, AS HIMSELF: It's so very precious for us to be able to do things when we choose to do them—not because somebody we love has to have it or because they are going to freak out or because they are going to keep talking at us until we do. People are very scared of spending so much of their lives having to give when it's not from the heart. So they're very reactive. He says, "Just get it! Just understand. I just do not want to do this today. I just need to protect my autonomy." From the tone of your boyfriend's voice when he says, "I just want you to get it," he has a serious case of the sick-of-dependency, not-yet-autonomous blues. So what do you say to him next?

PARTICIPANT I: I just rolled over and went to sleep. [Laughter.] Well, I kind of yelled and screamed, "No, no, no!" I got angry, really fierce, and said, "I'm very upset." And he said, "Oh, good, you've got life in you." [Laughter.] And then he got silent.

MARSHALL: You know that he was really scared. He doesn't feel he can protect himself against you. You were very tense, and he knows to withdraw and protect himself.

PARTICIPANT I: What can I do in this case? Just go "under the hat" with myself [give oneself empathy]?

MARSHALL: The most important thing, of course, is for you not to think that this has anything to do with you.

PARTICIPANT I: Yeah, I was okay with that.

MARSHALL: Then that's about the best I know to do in a situation when somebody says no to my needs: making sure I don't think there is anything wrong with my needs. I need to really work fast because, with that intensity and pain, I could make a mistake and think there is something wrong with my needs if they can scare a person that much.

PARTICIPANT I: Well, I just would have liked to have heard what he wanted.

MARSHALL: He is all tied up in protecting his autonomy—that's what he wants. He needs space to just feel safe in the relationship, to know he's not going to get sucked into something before he is ready.

PARTICIPANT I: So I can kind of give myself empathy silently. Keep quiet.

MARSHALL: Yeah. Just be aware that if he's like most men—if my wife is right—he'll need about three incarnations to get past that. [Laughter.]

So in the meantime, go and get some women friends and just don't aggravate yourself. My wife once said about the best one-liner I've ever heard; she said to me, "You could read demands into a rock." [Laughter.] I said, "Guilty as charged."

Do You Want to Hear This?

PARTICIPANT I: When he's having his sick-of-dependency and not-yet-autonomous blues, I get really desperate because I want him to know that, in fact, I can't make him do anything, so he doesn't need to worry about that at all. If he could just trust that, we could have a lot more fun. Do you hear what my pain is?

MARSHALL: Only when he feels that you can fully empathize with how frightening it is for him to be in a close relationship—and that might take a long time—then, maybe, he can start to understand how frustrating it is for you to have needs and not be able to express them without having him turn them into demands.

PARTICIPANT I: Is there some way I can effectively communicate to him how much I want him to understand that I can't make him do anything?

MARSHALL: You can try. This person will hear anything as a demand, even—or perhaps in particular—your silence, so you might as well have some fun screaming. If you keep your needs hidden inside, he's going to carry that as a very heavy burden. Screaming what you have to say a few thousand times might get him to understand.

PARTICIPANT I: I was concerned about doing the inner work on my own without saying anything to him, because he may be thinking I am avoiding the issue by not talking about it.

MARSHALL: Yes, how painful it is not to be able to voice our needs. There's nothing wrong with screaming, "I would like you to tell me what I have to do or say for you to trust that I never want to get you into anything that is painful for you," while also empathizing with just how frightened he may be having grown up in a family where he's been told he's wrong. He has been through all kinds of games, so he needs a lot of time and patience to gain that trust. I don't think it's going to happen just by your telling him that you won't ever make him do anything. He needs a lot of empathy due to the scare from his prior experiences.

Expressing Feelings and Needs

MARSHALL: Who's got another one?

PARTICIPANT J: It's a telephone call from my boyfriend. He says, "Hi, I'm not going to be able to come today. My daughter's school is getting out at 1:30, and I want to spend quality time with you, and I will be nervous if we get together."

MARSHALL: And then you say?

PARTICIPANT J: I was able to identify my feelings. "I have pain in my heart." That's what I said.

MARSHALL: "I have pain in my heart."

PARTICIPANT J: Yeah, but I wasn't able to identify my needs.

MARSHALL: But you weren't able to say what your needs were, and your timing was a bit judgmental. This person needs empathy, and the first thing they hear is "pain in your heart." So we already have a nice fight about to start here.

PARTICIPANT J: When I said I had pain in my heart, he asked, "Why?"

MARSHALL: I've asked people in several countries, "What are the hardest messages for you to hear and really feel safe?" "Why" questions top the list. If you really want to scare people, ask "why" questions. "Why?"

PARTICIPANT J: Silence, I said nothing. Then he listed a whole bunch of other reasons why he wasn't able to come.

MARSHALL: This poor suicidal guy. He doesn't realize that when he tries to explain and justify, it just sounds like an attack. So then what?

PARTICIPANT J: I said, "I have pain in my heart, and I have to think about that." And then I thought, "I am going to call some of my NVC friends."

MARSHALL: Ah, now there's a smart thing to do! Okay, so if I understand this, you really wanted to be with this person.

PARTICIPANT J: Yes.

MARSHALL: And this person's needs were in conflict with yours. This person was saying, "I have other needs right now, other than to meet your needs."

PARTICIPANT J: Right, and logically I could understand that, but in my heart . . .

MARSHALL: In your head you could understand it, but you have the pain in your heart because you heard what?

PARTICIPANT J: I heard, "I don't want to be with you."

MARSHALL: Yes, you heard a rejection. That's how to make life really miserable. When somebody's needs are in conflict with ours and that person says, "I'd like to do something else right now rather than meet your needs," you hear it as, "I don't want to be with you." You have nicer language; you say "pain in my heart." I must confess, I have been known to wear judging ears when I hear a *no* myself. It's very hard to put on NVC ears when you hear a *no*.

Yes, by all means, let's learn how to put on NVC ears in such a situation, because that can save us a lot of misery. If we hear another person's needs being different from ours as a rejection, we will soon be rejected. Who wants to be around people who read rejection each time your needs are in conflict with theirs? That gets very heavy very quickly. So unless we learn to put on NVC ears, we will, in fact, drive the other person away. I realize that this is not always easy, but we need to learn to put on NVC ears. [Marshall puts on a pair of fuzzy NVC ears. The audience chuckles. He responds to the laughter by saying:] I feel very hurt. [More laughter.]

PARTICIPANT J: Your ears aren't working then. [Lots more laughter.]

MARSHALL: Yes, these are faulty ears, obviously. I need to get another pair.

Now, as soon as I put on these ears, a miracle takes place: rejection vanishes from the earth. I never hear a *no*. I never hear a *don't want*. Judgments and criticism vanish from the earth. All I hear is the truth, which to an NVC-speaking person is this: "All that other people are ever expressing are their feelings and needs. The only things that people are ever saying, no matter how they are expressing it, are how they are and what they would like to make life even better. When people say no, that's just a poor way of letting us know what they really want. We don't want to make it worse by hearing a rejection; we hear what they want."

Some of you have heard me tell about the woman who said to her husband, "I don't want you spending so much time at work." Then she got furious with him when he signed up for a bowling league. [Laughter.] She had told him what she didn't want, and he didn't have NVC ears on. He didn't know how to hear what she did want. Of course, it would have made it easier if she had said what she did want. But if he had been wearing NVC ears, when she said, "I don't want you spending so much time at work," he would have said:

HUSBAND: Oh, so you're concerned about my well-being, and you want me to get more recreation?

WIFE: Not on your life. You have spent only two nights in the past six months with the children and me.

HUSBAND: Ah, so you're really disappointed in how much time we spend together, and you'd like me to spend at least one night a week with you and the children?

WIFE: Exactly.

You see, with NVC ears, we never hear what people don't want. We try to help them get clear about what they do want. Being clear only about what we don't want is a dangerous phenomenon. It gets us into all kinds of confusion.

When we are clear on what we do want from other people, especially when we are clear about what we want their reasons to be in doing something, then it becomes clear to us that we can never get our needs met through any kind of threats or punitive measures. Whether we are parents, teachers, or whatever, we never get our needs met by punishment. No one who is the least bit conscious is going to want anyone to do anything for us out of fear, guilt, or shame. We're NVC-oriented enough to see into the future, to see that any time anyone does anything out of fear, guilt, or shame, everybody loses. So we need to put the NVC ears on now and give this person some empathy. Let's try it again.

MARSHALL, AS BOYFRIEND: I have a real conflict. I would really like to be with you when I can be conscious and give you my full attention, but today my attention is distracted by my daughter.

PARTICIPANT J, AS HERSELF: Do you want me to be an NVCer?

MARSHALL, AS HIMSELF: Yeah, put these ears on. [He hands Participant J a pair of NVC ears, which she dons.]

PARTICIPANT J, AS NVCER: I'm really disappointed.

MARSHALL: No, no. This poor person needs empathy.

PARTICIPANT J, AS NVCER: So, you'd really like to spend some quality time with me, when you can be fully in my presence without distraction, but today you need to attend to your daughter because she's getting out of school early?

MARSHALL, AS BOYFRIEND: Yes, thank you for giving me that empathy. You see, I have this real fear that if I don't always meet the needs of the person I care for, then that person is going to take it as a rejection, and I'm going to be rejected and abandoned. So it's very terrifying for me to tell you that my needs are in conflict with yours. I've had terrible experiences like that in my background—when I don't do what everybody else wants, I don't get the love that I want. It's just terrifying for me to tell you that my needs are in conflict with yours. I was afraid you'd hear, "I don't want to be with you."

PARTICIPANT J, AS NVCER: You want some more empathy?

MARSHALL, AS BOYFRIEND: Yeah, I want some more empathy.

PARTICIPANT J, AS NVCER: I guess you were scared that you were not going to be able to spend time with me today because you're feeling a need to attend to your daughter. And you're afraid that by telling me that, I may think that you don't want to spend time with me. In the past, you've had many experiences and times when you wanted to fill the needs of others you care for, but when you had a conflict or hadn't been able to do that, they heard that you didn't want to spend time with them. When they felt rejected, they punished you, and then you felt guilt and shame. They judged you, and you felt even more guilty and scared.

MARSHALL, AS BOYFRIEND: Yes, yes—it feels so good to get this empathy—the heck with my daughter, I'm coming over! [Laughter and applause.] Now I can even hear you when you start to tell me about the pain in your heart, because I got my empathy first.

PARTICIPANT J, AS NVCER: I'm wondering if you'd like to hear how I'm feeling about this.

MARSHALL, AS BOYFRIEND: Yeah, I'd like to hear how you are feeling.

PARTICIPANT J, AS NVCER: I'm feeling really disappointed.

MARSHALL, AS BOYFRIEND: Oh, I'm sorry; I didn't mean to disappoint you.

MARSHALL, AS HIMSELF: Now watch out. He has learned suicidal tendencies to take responsibility for other people's feelings. As soon as she said she was disappointed, he went on alert. Without NVC, when people hear somebody in pain, immediately they feel that they have done something wrong and now they have to do something about it. And so this person is doing the number one thing that people unfamiliar with NVC do: apologize. You know that there is a judgment coming soon when you hear these words: "I'm sorry." Then he repeats a whole lot of excuses that you don't want to hear about why it's so important for him to be with the daughter today, leaving you in all that pain, not getting any empathy.

MARSHALL, AS BOYFRIEND: I'm sorry, I didn't mean to disappoint you, but this is the only day, blah, blah, blah, excuses, excuses, justification, *et cetera*. Phew! [Laughter.]

PARTICIPANT J, AS HERSELF: Is this empathy time?

MARSHALL, AS HIMSELF: No, scream in NVC! You gave him empathy; now get empathy back.

PARTICIPANT J, AS NVCER: Okay. Well, I'm having a need to share my feelings with you right now.

MARSHALL, AS BOYFRIEND: Yes, it's important that you do.

PARTICIPANT J, AS NVCER: What I'd like to do right now is tell you what I'm feeling, and then when I'm done, maybe you could tell me back what I've said?

MARSHALL, AS BOYFRIEND: Oh yes, I have a very bad habit; I don't listen very well. I've never been able to listen too well. My mother was not a very good listener either, and, uh, you know . . . [Laughter.]

PARTICIPANT J, AS HERSELF: Next time will I talk to his mom?

MARSHALL, AS HIMSELF: No, just scream in NVC.

PARTICIPANT J, AS NVCER: I hear that you have some pain around this.

MARSHALL, AS HIMSELF: No, don't give him even that much empathy; just scream in NVC.

PARTICIPANT J, AS NVCER: I have a need to share my feelings and my needs about this with you, and I would really like you to listen to what I have to say. And afterward I'd like you to tell me what I said. Okay?

MARSHALL, AS BOYFRIEND: Yeah. [Marshall shrugs his shoulders and rolls his eyes. The audience laughs.]

PARTICIPANT J, AS HERSELF: Did you talk to him ahead of time? [More laughter.]

MARSHALL, AS HIMSELF: I've even got his expressions down pat!

PARTICIPANT J, AS NVCER: I'm feeling really disappointed when I hear that you're not going to be able to spend the day with me.

MARSHALL, AS BOYFRIEND: Yes, but . . .

MARSHALL, PLAYING NVC COACH TO BOYFRIEND: Shh, shh, just hear her out.

MARSHALL, AS HIMSELF: Sometimes you need an emergency NVC coach to help out.

PARTICIPANT J, AS NVCER: I was really looking forward to spending the day with you because I enjoy your company so much, and I was needing to see you.

[Marshall enacts dialogue between judging puppet (boyfriend) and NVC puppet (coach).]

NVC COACH: Can you tell her back what she said?

BOYFRIEND: Yes, I understand how she feels.

NVC COACH: Could you just say what she feels?

BOYFRIEND: No, she's right—she has every right to feel that way. It was terrible of me. I should never have made the promise if I knew that I might not have been able to do it. It was terrible of me. I just feel terribly guilty.

NVC COACH: Are you aware that when you hear what she said as a judgment of yourself, that it is a further violation of her?

BOYFRIEND: Huh?

NVC COACH: When you're hearing what another person says as meaning you did something wrong, that's a further violation of the other person, because then not only is she not getting the understanding that she needs, but she also gets the feeling that her honesty creates problems for you. It's going to be harder for her to be honest in the future if she tries to tell you what's going on with her and you think you did something wrong.

BOYFRIEND: But I'm not wearing NVC ears; I can't hear anything except that I did something wrong.

NVC COACH: You want some NVC ears?

BOYFRIEND: Yes! [Laughter as Marshall puts NVC ears on the judging boyfriend puppet.]

BOYFRIEND: So you're really feeling disappointed because I . . .

NVC COACH: No, you didn't have the ears on straight. No, she's not feeling disappointed because of such and such. Quit taking responsibility for her feelings. Just hear what is going on in her.

MARSHALL, AS NVC BOYFRIEND: So you feel disappointed because you were looking forward to this, and you really wanted to spend that time with me.

PARTICIPANT J, AS NVCER: Yes!

MARSHALL, AS BOYFRIEND: [Hearing with new NVC ears.] It's something you were really looking forward to.

PARTICIPANT J, AS NVCER: Yeah. I really enjoyed hearing you say that!

MARSHALL, AS BOYFRIEND: It really feels good when you can get that empathy?

PARTICIPANT J, AS NVCER: Yes, it feels really good.

MARSHALL, AS BOYFRIEND: And you don't want me to feel like a worm?

PARTICIPANT J, AS NVCER: No, I don't want you to feel like a worm.

MARSHALL, AS BOYFRIEND: You just needed this empathy.

PARTICIPANT J, AS NVCER: Yeah!

MARSHALL, AS BOYFRIEND: And that's all I have to do?

PARTICIPANT J, AS NVCER: [With new softness in her voice.] Yes, and I'm feeling really grateful to you for hearing that.

MARSHALL, AS BOYFRIEND: That's amazing! I always thought that I had to do everything that everyone else wanted me to do in order to be loved. The idea that people just want my empathy and then my honesty— this is astonishing! Thank you for staying with me. I'll try to keep these ears on all the time.

PARTICIPANT J, AS NVCER: I'd enjoy that!

MARSHALL, AS HIMSELF: The first thing to do when we start to get angry or defensive is to recognize that we didn't hear the other person. What breaks us out of these fights is our consciousness. If we hear anything but a gift in the other person's message, then we didn't hear that person. You have to notice when your NVC ears have fallen off. Anger is a wonderful clue; it's like a wake-up call to an NVCer. As soon as I get angry or defensive or hear an attack or demand, I know that I didn't hear the other person. Instead of connecting to what's going on in them, I'm up in my head judging that they're wrong in some way. If I'm using NVC, I know to shut up as quickly as possible, put my NVC ears on, and listen to myself. I've wounded myself if I have judging ears. How do I do this?

I listen to myself. I give myself empathy. I see how much pain I've created for myself by putting on my judging ears and hearing all of that. I notice that this has happened, and then I shut up and enjoy the show going on in my head. It's just like watching a movie. [Laughter.]

Reassurance

PARTICIPANT K: I need to know the difference between empathizing with someone by saying, "It sounds like you're scared and need some reassurance" and actually reassuring them. What if they say, "Yes, I do need some reassurance"?

MARSHALL: If they say they want reassurance, and I can give it to them willingly, there's no problem. The problem is giving that reassurance when they want empathy. For example, one time my oldest daughter was looking in the mirror, and she said, "I'm as ugly as a pig." I said, "You're the most gorgeous creature God ever put on the face of this earth." She said, "Daddy!" and she stormed out and slammed the door. I was being judgmental there. She wanted empathy, and in order to meet my own needs, I tried to fix her.

What did I do? I went into the other room after judging myself a bit, saying, "You preach about this every day of the year, and then when it happens, you forget. You forget the Buddha's advice: 'Don't fix it, just be there.'" After that, I went to her and said,

MARSHALL: I'm guessing you needed to hear how disappointed you were with your appearance and not my reassurances.

DAUGHTER: That's right. You're always try to fix everything. [Laughter.]

MARSHALL: Guilty as charged.

Talking About It in Public

PARTICIPANT L: Sometimes I feel like I'm taking care of my mate's feelings. In the past I'd sometimes say something that he considered private or personal to another couple or in a group. I've since gotten clear on the difference between his stuff and my stuff, but occasionally there is a fine line between what I can and can't say. So I'm wondering, when we are in a group of people, when would it be appropriate and not "codependent" to ask him, "Is it okay if I talk about this?" Sometimes when I ask and he says no or says I shouldn't have said something, I feel angry and censored. Do you get my question?

MARSHALL: I think I do. Let me see. You're saying that sometimes it's not clear to you when your mate is comfortable with your talking about things with other people and when he's not.

PARTICIPANT L: Yeah.

MARSHALL: You've put your question in a non-NVC form and are heading in a direction that is dangerous. I cleaned it up for you and translated it into NVC. In the book *The Revolution in Psychiatry,* Ernest Becker, an anthropologist, suggested that depression results from cognitively arrested alternatives. He meant that by asking questions of the sort you started with, we fill our head with unanswerable questions. "Is it okay?" "Is it appropriate?" Those questions usually cannot be answered, and we end up spinning in our heads. Notice that I translated those questions. You're saying that sometimes your partner is uncomfortable with some things you say. It doesn't mean it's not okay for you to say those things. It doesn't mean that it's inappropriate. It just means he doesn't like it. You're just asking your partner, "I'm not clear what those things are. Can you give me an example of some of the things that you would like or wouldn't like for me to say?"

MARSHALL, AS PARTNER: Well, obviously I don't want you to say inappropriate things to other people. [Laughter.]

MARSHALL, AS HIMSELF: We need to get clear on the difference between emotional slavery, obnoxiousness, and liberation. Emotional slavery is as far from NVC as you can get—it's when people think they have to do everything that others think is appropriate, right, normal. These people spend all their lives thinking they have to please others and to guess what others think is appropriate. This is a heavy load. For example, someone comes home upset about something; it doesn't make any difference what it is.

PARTNER: I'm upset about everything.
JUDGING PERSON: Oh, here, eat some chicken soup.

MARSHALL: You see, it doesn't matter what it is. As soon as a person is in pain, then the other thinks they have to scurry around and take care of that person. Then they come to an NVC workshop where maybe I'm not totally coherent in explaining how we are not responsible for other people's feelings—I fail to make clear what we are responsible for. So they go home from the workshop, and when their partner says, "I'm still upset about A," they respond, "Well, that's your problem; I'm not responsible for your feelings." [Laughter.]

PARTNER: Where did you learn that?

NVC PARTICIPANT: At an NVC workshop.

PARTNER: I'm going to go kill those people!

MARSHALL: The NVC concept is: No, we are not responsible for other people's feelings, but we're conscious that we don't have to keep rebelling against them, saying things like, "I'm not responsible for your feelings." We can just hear what others are feeling and not lose our center. We can hear what they want and give them empathy, but we don't have to do what they want. We make it clear that we need empathy, not that we need them to give up or give in. To hear and respect what they need doesn't mean we must do what they ask.

Does that answer your question, or did I go astray? You need to get very clear on what you need. Without NVC, we say, "May I?" "Is it okay?" NVCers never want approval from other people. NVCers never give that power away and have other people tell them what to do.

This is what we'd say in NVC: "Here's what I want. I'd like to know where you stand in relationship to that. I want to know your needs as well as mine—not because when I hear your needs, I am going to give mine up or give in. I am conscious that I cannot benefit at your expense. Your needs are equally as important to me as my needs. And I'm clear that doesn't ever mean having to give up my needs."

I Lose Myself Around You

PARTICIPANT M: Are you ready for another one? She said, "I can't be in a long-term relationship. I lose myself around you. I'm not emotionally mature enough. I can see now that I was undergoing aberrant behavior in getting involved and agreeing to your wanting a long-term relationship. Something was wrong with me that led me to think that I could so quickly fall in love." I told her, "I'd still like to be your friend." And she said, "I don't know what to say."

MARSHALL: Yes, yes. This person has been taught non-NVC concepts of love, such as, "If you really love somebody, you deny your needs and take care of them." As soon as people like this get into a close relationship—a loving relationship—they turn judgmental. Until then, they're lovely; they're wonderful. These are the most dangerous judges, because they're really judges in NVC clothing. [Laughter.] You see, in the early stage of the relationship, they are giving from the heart; they enjoy giving. It's easy; they don't think of it until they pass the line.

What is the line? It's when people fear that they've "made a commitment." If you really want to scare them to death, talk about commitment, or use the word *serious*. As soon as they think it's a "serious relationship" or the word *love* comes up—"I love this person"—you're going to get killed. The moment they define it as a serious relationship, that's when they feel like they are responsible for your feelings. For to show love, they have to deny themselves and do for you.

All of that is behind the statements "I lose myself in a relationship with you. I can't stand it. I see your pain, and I lose me, and I need to get away from it all." At least they are taking responsibility for it. At a more primitive level, they would have put it all on you: "You're too dependent. You're too needy." That's seriously deranged. They are not aware of their own internal dynamic.

MARSHALL, AS PARTNER: I'm really scared to be in the relationship because I just close down. As soon as I see that you have any need or any pain, I just can't tell you the pain that I feel, and then I start to feel like I'm in prison. I feel like I'm being smothered, and so I just have to get out of this relationship as soon as possible.

MARSHALL, AS NVCER: As an NVCer, I have to do a lot of work with that, but I don't think there is something wrong with my needs or my love. If I did, that would make a bad situation doubly bad. I need not take responsibility for this. I need to truly hear what you are saying.

So you're in a panic. It's very hard for you to hold on to the deep caring and love that we've had without making of it responsibility and duty and obligation, closing down your own freedom, and feeling like you have to take care of me.

PARTICIPANT M, TAKING OVER AS PARTNER: Exactly! It's just like a prison. I can hardly breathe.

MARSHALL, AS NVCER: As soon as you hear my pain or my feelings, it's as if your life stops.

PARTICIPANT M, AS PARTNER: Yeah! [Sighs.]

MARSHALL, AS NVCER: I'm really glad you are telling me this. Would it be safer if we defined ourselves as friends rather than lovers?

PARTICIPANT M, AS PARTNER: No . . . I do this with friends, I do it with anybody I care for. I did this with my dog once. [Laughter.]

MARSHALL, AS NVCER: Gosh, I'm in such a dilemma here. I'd like to express my pain in relationship to that, but then if I express my pain, I'm afraid you'll freak.

PARTICIPANT M, AS PARTNER: Yes, I will. I will. As soon as you express any pain, I will think that I have done something wrong and that I have to do something about it. My life is over; I have to take care of you.

MARSHALL, AS NVCER: Then to myself I say, "Wow, how painful it is for me not to be able to get any empathy. To have someone receive my feelings and needs—all that is alive in me—that I would like to be a gift to someone; turning my needs into demands is painful to me. I do not know how to get what I need from this person. Let me try one more time to see if I can get empathy from this person."

Would you be willing to try to hear just one message from me without taking responsibility for it?

PARTICIPANT M, AS PARTNER: What do you mean?

MARSHALL, AS NVCER: I'd like to tell you a feeling and a need and have you hear only that and nothing else. Not to hear that you have to do anything about it. Not to hear that you did anything wrong. Just repeat back what you hear me say. Would you be willing to do that?

PARTICIPANT M, AS PARTNER: I'll try.

MARSHALL, AS NVCER: I feel so sad . . .

PARTICIPANT M, AS PARTNER: I'm sorry. [Laughter.]

MARSHALL, AS NVCER: Please don't. Just wait, hold on, and repeat what I say. I feel sad because I would like my feelings and my needs to be gifts to you and not a threat. Could you tell me what you heard me say?

PARTICIPANT M, AS PARTNER: That I shouldn't react so strongly.

MARSHALL, AS NVCER: No, I'm really not trying to tell you what you should or shouldn't do. I have a feeling and a need—just concentrate on that. I feel very sad because I would like my feelings and my needs to be a gift to you and not such a threat. Can you tell me what you heard me say?

PARTICIPANT M, AS PARTNER: That I make you sad.

MARSHALL, AS NVCER: You don't make me sad; my needs make me sad. Can you just hear that?

PARTICIPANT M, AS PARTNER: Say it again.

MARSHALL, AS NVCER: I feel very sad because I would really like it if my feelings and needs could be a gift to you and not a threat.

PARTICIPANT M, AS PARTNER: You feel sad because I—

MARSHALL, AS NVCER: No!

PARTICIPANT M, AS PARTNER: Because you?

MARSHALL, AS NVCER: Thank you.

PARTICIPANT M, AS PARTNER: Because you would like your feelings and needs to be a gift to me and not a threat.

MARSHALL, AS NVCER: I'm grateful that you heard that. Go in peace, and I hope some day you can come back and enjoy me.

Making a Request

PARTICIPANT M: But there's the next sentence. [Laughter.]

MARSHALL: What's that?

PARTICIPANT M: I want to say, "I feel scared; I need to feel we are still connected because we were connected. It doesn't necessarily matter how we are connected. I don't need you as a special partner, but I still need to feel we are connected and that we are friends."

MARSHALL: That's wonderful as far as you've gone, but if you stop there, it's not NVC. What you've stated is your feeling and your unmet need to still maintain contact with her, but you didn't make clear at the very end exactly what you want the other person to do. For a person who hears the way this one does, that will be fuel to the fire. When you say to a person without NVC ears, "Be a friend," and you don't make it clear what you are wanting from them, they'll read in again: "You want to smother me. You want me to be your slave." You must be very concrete with people who don't speak NVC. You cannot say, "I want you to love me. I want your understanding. I need you to listen. I need you to be a friend." Concretely, what exactly do you want this person to do to be your friend?

PARTICIPANT M: "I would like to call you at least once a month and check in on how you are and let you know how I am."

MARSHALL: What you need to say right now is, "I'd like you to tell me if you would be willing to have me call once a month to check in."

MARSHALL, AS PARTNER: For how many minutes?

PARTICIPANT M: Oh, about thirty minutes on a Sunday.

MARSHALL, AS PARTNER: Yes.

MARSHALL, AS HIMSELF: We need to be that concrete with NVC.

Dealing with Sexism or Racism

PARTICIPANT N: [Speaking softly.] I know someone who said that when a woman gets married, she turns into a bitch.

MARSHALL: Now, without NVC, we would quickly interpret that as a sexist remark. However, with such a thought in our head, we lose the power to get this person to be more sensitive to our needs. As soon as we judge someone as "sexist" or "racist"—even if we don't say the judgment out loud, but just carry it in our head—we have almost no power to get what we need. And what did you say next?

PARTICIPANT N: I paused because I was upset and didn't know what to say. I didn't tell him it was a sexist comment. During the pause, I felt the pain of men telling women things like that, and I wasn't in the mood to use NVC.

MARSHALL: That few-second pause used up all your NVC energy. Then you gave yourself permission to not use NVC.

PARTICIPANT N: I shook my head and said, "Women should have permission to be bitchy."

MARSHALL: You're agreeing. An NVCer never agrees or disagrees. I warn you: never go up to others' heads—it's ugly up there. [Laughter.] Stay away from their heads. Let's go to their hearts.

MARSHALL, AS MAN: Is it true that all you women turn into bitches when you get married?

MARSHALL, AS NVCER: [Silence.]

MARSHALL, AS HIMSELF: This is the pause. The NVCer is very angry right now. As I told you earlier, when NVCers get angry, they know that they didn't hear what they needed to hear. So this NVCer sits back and enjoys the judgment show that is going on in her head for a few moments.

> NVCER [INTERNAL DIALOGUE]: I'd like to take his sexist neck and wring it. I'm sick and tired of these remarks. I'm sick and tired of what I call insensitivity to my needs. Why, just because I am a woman, do I have to have this kind of talk thrown at me at work all the time? [Sigh.]
>
> NVCER [OUT LOUD]: Are you feeling some tension about things going on in your marriage that you want to talk about? [Lots of laughter.]

PARTICIPANT N: Actually, I really thought that at the time, but I didn't choose to bring that up, because we were having a farewell lunch for one of the employees at work.

MARSHALL, AS MAN: What are you talking about? We were just having fun. You take everything so sensitively.

MARSHALL, AS NVCER: So you were just playing with me and would have liked me to be able to enjoy that?

MARSHALL, AS MAN: Yeah.

MARSHALL, AS NVCER: Well, I'd like to tell you why that is not easy for me to do. I'd like to tell you how painful it is when I hear comments like that.

MARSHALL, AS MAN: Well, you shouldn't be so sensitive.

MARSHALL, AS NVCER: I'd like you to wait until I finish talking before you jump in and tell me what I shouldn't do. Would you be willing to do that?

MARSHALL, AS MAN: Touchy, touchy! [Laughter.]

MARSHALL, AS NVCER: So you're really feeling hurt, and you would like me to be able to play with you?

MARSHALL, AS MAN: Yeah—you liberals are really a pain in the ass to be around.

MARSHALL, AS NVCER: So you would like to be able to just joke and play and not have to worry about every word?

MARSHALL, AS MAN: Yeah.

MARSHALL, AS NVCER: And I'd like to be able to do that too, but I'd like you to understand why that is so painful for me to do. I'd like you to tell me if you would be willing to hear what goes on in me.

MARSHALL, AS HIMSELF: So now I educate him.

Name-calling

PARTICIPANT O: How does an NVCer react to forceful name-calling?

MARSHALL: In NVC, all names are tragic expressions of unmet needs. An NVCer asks himself, when the names are coming at him, "What are they wanting that they are not getting?" Tragically, name-callers don't know any other way of saying the need except to call the name.

NAME-CALLER: You're too sensitive!

NVCER: You would like me to understand you differently?

NAME-CALLER: You're the most selfish person I've ever met.

NVCER: You would have liked me to save that last piece of cake for you?

Names are simply tragic expressions of unmet needs. NVCers know there is no such thing as normal, abnormal, right, wrong, good, or bad. They know that all of those are a product of language that has trained people to live under a king. If you want to train people to be docile to a higher authority, to fit into hierarchical structures in a subservient way, it is very important to get people up in their head and to get them thinking what is "right," what is "normal," what is "appropriate," and to give that power to an authority at the top who defines what those are. You can get my booklet on social change if you want to learn more about how this came about.

When people are raised in that culture, they have this tragic trick played on them. When they are hurting the most and needing the most, they don't know how to express it except by calling other people names.

With NVC, we want to break that cycle. We know that the basis of violence is when people are in pain and don't know how to say that clearly. There is a book called *Out of Weakness,* by Andrew Schmookler. He writes that violence—whether we are talking about verbal, psychological, or physical violence between husband and wife, parents and children, or nations—at its base is people not knowing how to get in touch with what is inside. Instead, they are taught a language that indicates that there are villains out there, bad guys out there, who are causing the problem. Then you have a country where even the leader will say of another country, "They're the evil empire." And then the leaders of the other country will say back, "These are imperialist oppressors," instead of seeing and revealing the pain, fear, and unmet needs behind the other's words. This is a very dangerous social phenomenon. That's why NVCers are committed to just hearing the pain and needs behind any name—not to take it in and not to respond in kind.

EXPRESSING APPRECIATION

PARTICIPANT P: Could you please say the three things that you need in order to express appreciation?

MARSHALL: There are three things we need to express appreciation—not praise, because there is no such thing as praise in NVC. Praise is a classic judging technique; managers love it because they say research shows that employees perform better if you praise them at least once a day. Praise does work for a while, until the employees see the manipulation in it. We never give appreciation in NVC to try to create some result in other people. We only give it to celebrate, to let them know how great we feel about something that they have done. The three things are:

- What the other person has done that we appreciate, and we are very specific about that
- Our feelings
- Our needs that have been fulfilled

WHAT DOES IT TAKE TO PRACTICE NVC?

PARTICIPANT Q: I would also like you to mention the three things that it takes to become proficient at NVC.

MARSHALL: First of all, the good news is that it doesn't require us to be perfect. It does not require us to be saints. And we don't have to be patient. We don't have to have positive self-esteem; we don't have to have self-confidence. I have demonstrated that you don't even have to be a normal person. [Laughter.]

What does it take? First and foremost, it takes spiritual clarity. We have to be highly conscious of how we want to connect with human beings. We're living in a society, I'm afraid to say, that is largely judgmental in its history and evolution. It's leaning toward NVC—and very rapidly if you think like Teilhard de Chardin. (He was a paleontologist who thought in terms of tens of thousands of years.) But it's not moving as fast as I'd like, so I'm doing what I can to speed it up.

The main thing I'm trying to do is work on myself. When I get myself fully engaged with NVC, I think I am helping the planet; then what energy I have left over, I use to try to help other people become engaged with NVC. So the most important thing is spiritual clarity—that we be highly conscious of how we want to connect with people. For me, I have to stop every day—two, three, four times—really stop and remind myself how I want to connect with other people in this world.

How do I do that? This is individual for everyone. Some people call it meditation, prayer, stopping and slowing down—whatever you call it. I do it differently every day myself, but it's basically just stopping and slowing down and doing a check on what is running through my head. Are judgments running through my head? Is NVC running through my head? I stop and look at what is going on in my head, and I slow down. I remind myself of the "subtle sneaky important reason I was born a human being and not a chair," to use a line from one of my favorite plays, *A Thousand Clowns.* So that's the most important thing: spiritual clarity.

Second: practice, practice, practice. I make a note every time I catch myself judging myself or other people. I make a note of what the stimulus was for this. What did I do? What did others say or do that, all of a sudden, I gave myself permission to turn back into judgment? Then I use that. Some time in the day, I sit and look at my list, and I try to give myself empathy for the pain that was going on in me at the time. I try not to beat myself up. I try to hear what pain was going on in me that led me to speak in that way. Then I ask myself, "How could I have used NVC in that situation? What might the other person have been feeling and needing?"

Now, NVCers love to mess things up, because an NVCer doesn't try to be perfect. We know the danger of trying to be perfect. We just try to become progressively less stupid. [Laughter.] When your objective is to become progressively less stupid, every time you mess something up, it becomes cause for a celebration. It gives you a chance to learn how to be less stupid. So practice, practice, practice learning how to be less stupid.

And third, it really helps to be part of an NVC support community. We are living in a judgmental world, and it helps to create an NVC world around us from which we can start to build a greater world—an NVC world. That is why I am so grateful that we have all of the NVC teams locally.

WHAT'S LOVE GOT TO DO WITH IT?

It may help you to understand that Nonviolent Communication grew from my attempt to understand the concept of love and how to manifest it, how to *do* it. I had come to the conclusion that love is not just something we feel, but something we manifest, something we do, something we have. And *love is something we give.* We give of ourselves in particular ways. It's a gift when you reveal yourself nakedly and honestly, at any given moment, for no other purpose than to reveal what's alive in you. Not to blame, criticize, or punish—just "Here I am, and here is what I would like. This is my vulnerability at this moment." To me, that giving is a manifestation of love.

Another way we give of ourselves is through how we receive another person's message. It's a gift to receive it empathically, connecting with what's alive in that person, making no judgment. It's a gift when we try to hear what is alive in the other person and what that person would like. So Nonviolent Communication is just a manifestation of what I understand love to be. In that way, it's similar to the Judeo-Christian concepts of "Love your neighbor as yourself" and "Judge not lest you be judged."

It's amazing what happens when we connect with people in this way. This beauty, this power connects us with an energy that I choose to call Beloved Divine Energy—one of the many names for God. So Nonviolent Communication helps me stay connected with that beautiful Divine Energy within myself and to connect with it in others. It's the closest thing to "love" I've ever experienced.

CONCLUSION

In relationships, we want to be ourselves, but we want to do that in a way that is respectful to others, even if they're not treating us in a particularly respectful way. We want to connect with them, yet we don't want to get caught up in their way of doing business. So how do we do both? I'm suggesting that we do that by expressing ourselves very assertively. NVC is a very assertive language. We can be very loud and clear about what we feel, what our needs are, what we want from the other person. However, we're very assertive without doing two things that turn assertiveness into violence. In NVC, we assert ourselves but without criticizing the other. We say nothing in the language of NVC that in any way implies that the other person is ever wrong. By wrong, I mean about a thousand different things—inappropriate, selfish, insensitive—in fact, any word that classifies or categorizes what the other person is.

So, in NVC we learn how to be very assertive about saying what's going on in us, and we also have the wonderful art when we speak NVC of very assertively telling people what we would like them to do. But we present this to them as a request and not as a demand. Because at the moment people hear from our lips anything that sounds like a criticism or a demand, or if it sounds somehow to them like we don't value their needs equal to our needs—when others get the impression that we are only out to get our way—we lose, because then they have less energy to sincerely consider our needs. Most of their energy will go into defensiveness or resistance.

We want to be very assertive when we speak NVC—to speak it in a way that gives others our assertiveness as a gift that reveals nakedly what's going on in us, that clearly tells them what we would like from them.

I would say the basic human need, the thing that is the greatest feeling for everybody universally, is the joy we feel when we see we have the power to enrich life. I have never met a person who doesn't enjoy giving to other people, provided it's done willingly. I believe this happens once others trust that I am not trying to coerce them into doing anything and we can keep an NVC dance going in which we both continue to share what we both feel and need. And I have every hope that this is happening. In my relationships, I get to test out this rosy philosophy quite a bit.

3

GETTING PAST THE PAIN BETWEEN US

Healing and Reconciliation
without Compromise

The following is excerpted from a workshop I gave on October 4, 2002. "Getting Past the Pain" focuses on mending our relationships with one another and gives us skills for understanding and resolving our conflicts, for healing old hurts, and for developing satisfying relationships using NVC.

In this chapter, you will find steps you can take for healing or reconciling any conflicted relationship—whether at work, at home, at school, or in your community. It will also give you a sense of the energy of empathy: the compassion and the heartfelt "presence" necessary for healing to take place. Nonviolent Communication skills empower you to make lasting peace and even to prevent trouble from happening in the first place. Join this dialogue and enjoy the magic that understanding brings when we listen and speak from the heart.

The training opens with me role-playing a situation posed by an audience member.

HEALING BITTERNESS

MARSHALL: What can I share with you about healing and reconciliation that would meet your needs? What would you like to hear me talk about? Or maybe you have some pain left over from something that happened to you in the past with somebody, and you would like us to do it "live" and not just talk about it?

PARTICIPANT R: I wonder how I can get past or release a lot of bitterness I have toward somebody.

MARSHALL: How about if I use Nonviolent Communication and play the role of the person you have the bitterness toward? I'll be that person, but I'm going to be speaking to you as someone living Nonviolent Communication. All you need to do is just say what you want to say. Okay, you got the game? Good, now who am I going to be?

PARTICIPANT R: My brother.

MARSHALL, AS BROTHER: Sister, I am very touched that you want to heal this bitterness between us and by the courage you're showing. What would be a big gift to me is if you would share what is alive with you right now in relationship to me. Just say what's going on, however you want to.

PARTICIPANT R: I have a real ethical problem with you. You weren't honest with me or reliable when our parents were declining. When I reached out to you to try and work it out, you were unwilling. You just wanted to put the past behind us. That's what you've always done, our whole life. You say it's my problem; you don't want to deal with it. Whatever is upsetting to me doesn't seem to matter.

MARSHALL, AS BROTHER: You've said a lot to me here, a lot of different feelings. Let me check to be sure I understand fully. I'm hearing a lot of anger connecting to a need you may have had for more support when our parents were declining. Did I hear that much right?

PARTICIPANT R: Yes.

MARSHALL, AS BROTHER: So that was real, and you'd like some understanding now about how difficult this was for you to go through, how you would've really loved support. But not only didn't you get the support that you would've liked, I'm also hearing that some of the things I did since then in relationship to family matters have left you with a great deal of pain—that you would have really liked us to have made those decisions differently.

PARTICIPANT R: Yeah.

MARSHALL, AS BROTHER: Yeah, especially since it wasn't the only time you've experienced that your own needs weren't given the consideration you would've liked. Did I hear your message accurately?

PARTICIPANT R: Yeah, yeah.

MARSHALL, AS BROTHER: Do you like me when I'm wearing empathy ears?

PARTICIPANT R: Yes! Will you be my brother?

MARSHALL, AS BROTHER: So, still wearing these ears, I'd like to hear whatever else is still alive, still going on in you.

PARTICIPANT R: You say you want us to get back together, but I just can't. We just don't resolve conflicts in the family, and I don't want to live like that any more.

MARSHALL, AS BROTHER: So, if I hear your need, it's to protect yourself from the pain that you've felt in the past when you've reached out and tried to resolve things and it didn't happen. At this point you've had enough of that. It's as if part of you would like to hear from me, but not if it means going through the pain that you've felt in the past.

PARTICIPANT R: Right. I'm still left in a quandary, because I can't see it working either way. If I go back, it's not going to be good for me, but then just staying away seems unnatural.

MARSHALL, AS BROTHER: So you're really torn. You have two needs. One need is for there to be reconciliation and healing between us. The other is this strong need to protect yourself. You don't know how to meet both needs.

PARTICIPANT R: Right.

MARSHALL, AS BROTHER: That's a really painful conflict.

PARTICIPANT R: Right.

MARSHALL, AS BROTHER: Anything else, Sister, that you'd like me to hear before I react to what you've said?

PARTICIPANT R: No.

MARSHALL, AS BROTHER: Hearing you now, with these empathy ears on, I feel a deep, deep sadness, because I can see that I have not met my own needs with some of the things that I've done in our relationship: my need to nurture you in the way that I'd like, to contribute to your well-being. When I see how my actions have just the opposite effect, how they've created so much pain for you, I feel a deep sadness, and I'm very vulnerable right now. I'd like to hear how you feel when I tell you about this sadness.

PARTICIPANT R: You're probably in the same quandary that I am, in the sense that you don't know how to meet my needs without being highly uncomfortable yourself.

MARSHALL, AS BROTHER: I want to thank you for anticipating that. What I'd really like right now is for you to just hear how sad I feel that I didn't get my need met to contribute to your well-being as I would've liked.

PARTICIPANT R: I appreciate that.

MARSHALL, AS BROTHER: Now, what I would like to do is tell you what was going on in me when I did those things in our relationship. And—I think you've already somewhat anticipated this—I'd like to make it as clear as I can. First, about not providing more support for your efforts in dealing with the stress around our parents when they were declining: I had an inner message telling me that I really should help and that I was a rat for not giving more support. And then because I was feeling so guilty, I wasn't able to hear your pain and your needs with my compassionate listening ears. Your requests were sounding too much like a demand on me. I was torn because I wanted to help, but I was also angry hearing a demand. I felt guilty, and I just didn't know how to handle all of those feelings going on in me except to try to avoid the whole issue. I'd like to know how you feel when I tell you that.

PARTICIPANT R: It makes sense . . . clarifies things.

MARSHALL, AS BROTHER: So then, just as you have some hurt in relationship to me, I have some hurt that I haven't known how to express to you about things that have happened in the past. I wish I could've known how to talk about it, but having that hurt inside and not knowing how to express it made it come out angry toward you at times. I wish I could have expressed it differently. So how do you feel when I tell you that?

PARTICIPANT R: Good to hear.

MARSHALL, AS BROTHER: Is there anything else that you'd like me to hear, or that you want to say, or that you want to hear from me?

PARTICIPANT R: I guess I'd want to know how to work through this in a way that is comfortable enough for each of us. Then we can move forward. It's a mess that has to be cleaned up. And I'm willing to hear whatever you have to say, to open the dialogue.

MARSHALL, AS BROTHER: I have an idea. Tell me how this feels to you: how about asking the folks who are recording this workshop to send me a copy of this as a start? And then maybe call me and ask me if I'd like to continue this kind of dialogue, maybe with the help of a third party?

PARTICIPANT R: Yeah, I think that's an excellent idea.

MARSHALL, AS BROTHER: Okay, let's do it.

PARTICIPANT R: Thank you.

Reactions to the Role-Play

MARSHALL: Okay, any reactions to that situation? Questions?

PARTICIPANT S: What would you recommend in the event that sending the tape was not a possibility?

MARSHALL: I think we got some of the healing accomplished that Participant R wanted, that we dealt with the hurt. Now she wants to deepen the relationship. That shows that she doesn't have to have her brother physically available to get some healing. Sure, it would be nice now to deepen things with him and go further, but she doesn't need to depend on his availability for her own healing to take place. We don't need the other person for healing to take place—especially if that person is not alive any more or is inaccessible. Fortunately, we can heal *fully* without the other person being involved.

PARTICIPANT S: It seems to me to be very important, if I have an issue with a person that I cannot heal by myself, to have somebody who is able to play the NVC part with me—like you did right now—someone who is able to listen to my issues and listen empathically. So my question is, if I don't have that friend, do you have a method to do that with myself?

MARSHALL: Yes, I think you can do it with yourself. Certainly, in the best of all worlds in the previous example, we would have had the brother here. That would have been even more powerful. He could have played himself. But we can do it without him.

Let me clarify one of the important principles we use to do that: it's very important to notice in the role-play how little we talked about the past. Sister made very brief reference to what I, the brother, did, but we didn't go into detail. What I've found over the years is the more we talk about the past, the less we heal from it. Most of the role-play conversation was about what was alive in both of us right now. We talked about the present—what she's still feeling as a result of what happened in the past.

Most people think you have to understand the past to get healing and that you have to tell the story to get the understanding. They mix up intellectual understanding with empathy. Empathy is where the healing comes from. Telling the story does give intellectual understanding about why the person did it, but that's not empathy, and it doesn't do any healing. In fact, retelling the story can deepen the pain. It's like reliving the pain again.

So though we did not deny the past, and we did make reference to what the brother had done, we didn't go into the details. We didn't say, for example, "I had to take Mother to all the stores, and not only that, but when Dad got sick, you know, blah, blah, blah." The more she would've talked about that, the less healing would've happened. Especially when you do it with the people you have pain about. They're not going to see that your objective is to get understanding for the pain. They're going to think your objective is to create a case to send them to hell.

PARTICIPANT S: I was kind of getting the feeling that the brother had issues that he hadn't expressed to her. What if he's holding stuff against her?

MARSHALL: As the brother, at the end I said, "I'm feeling some hurt that I don't know how to express to you." That's all I need to do. I said that I was still feeling some hurt in relationship to the past for which I needed some understanding. But that understanding didn't mean that I had to tell the story, to talk more about the past. It just meant I got it back from her. I saw in her eyes that she had heard it.

THE FIRST STAGE OF HEALING: EMPATHIC CONNECTION

MARSHALL: So, what we first want to remember, whether we want to heal ourselves or we want to help somebody else heal, is to put the *focus on what's alive now,* not on what happened in the past. If there is a discussion of the past, say five words, no more: "when you ran away from home," "when you hit me," whatever. The first stage of healing involves empathizing with what's alive right now in relationship to what happened. In my role as brother, I *empathically connected* to what is alive in her now. Doing that requires certain things.

The first step to empathic connection is what Martin Buber called the most precious gift one human being can give to another: presence. In the role of the brother, I was fully present to what was alive in her now, in this moment. I wasn't thinking of what I was going to say next or what had happened in the past.

This is a hard gift to give to somebody, because it means that I can bring nothing in from the past. Even a diagnosis I've had of this person in the past will get in the way of empathy. This is why my clinical training in psychoanalysis was a deficit. It taught me how to sit and think about what the person was saying and how to intellectually interpret it, but not how to be fully present to this person, which is really where healing comes from. To be fully present, I have to throw out all of my clinical training, all of my diagnoses, all of this prior knowledge about human beings and their development. All of that only gives me intellectual understanding, which blocks empathy.

The best I can tell you about what empathy feels like to me is that it's like riding a surfboard. You're trying to get with the energy of the wave, trying to hear what's alive right now. I'm trying to go with the rhythm of life that's in this person. And sometimes just by looking at the floor I can get more with it than looking at the person and being distracted by things.

PARTICIPANT S: I get sucked into sympathy, though.

Empathy Versus Sympathy

MARSHALL: Sympathy, empathy—let's get clear about the difference. If I have strong feelings in me, just being conscious of them is sympathy, not empathy. So, if I had been the brother and I had said, "Boy, I feel sad when you say that," that would have been sympathy, not empathy. Remember a time when you had a pain in your body, maybe a headache or a toothache, and you got into a good book? What happened to the pain? You weren't aware of it. The pain was there—I mean, the physical condition hadn't changed—but you weren't home. You were out visiting. That's empathy. You were visiting the book.

With empathy, we're with the other person's feelings. That doesn't mean we feel their feelings. We're just with them while they are feeling those feelings. Now, if I take my mind away from them for one second, I may notice I have strong feelings of my own. If so, I don't try to push my feelings down. My feelings are telling me I'm not with the other person, that I'm home again. So I say to myself, "Go back to them."

However, if my pain is too great, I can't empathize. So I might say, "I'm in so much pain right now hearing some things you've said, I'm not able to listen. Could we give me a few moments to deal with that so that I can go back to hearing you?"

It's important not to mix up empathy and sympathy, because when someone is in pain and then I say, "Oh, I understand how you feel, and I feel so sad about that," I take the flow away from them and bring their attention over to me.

I sometimes use a phrase that many people hate about Nonviolent Communication—I say that empathy requires "learning how to enjoy another person's pain." Now, why do I use such a sick phrase? When I used to come to San Diego, a friend of mine would call me on the phone and say, "Come over and play with my pain." She knew that I knew what she meant by that. She was dying of a very painful disease, and she used to tell me that what made it even worse was having to deal with other people's reactions to her pain. Their response coming out of their good, sympathetic hearts was creating so much of a problem for her that she would rather be alone with her pain than have to end up taking care of other people around it. And so she said, "That's why I like to call you, Marshall, because you're so coldhearted. You're such a miserable son of a bitch. I know I can talk with you, and you're not going to give a damn about anybody but yourself."

She knew I could understand "idiomatic NVC." And she knew that I considered it a pleasure in the sense that whether others are experiencing pain or joy, when we are present to them in a certain way, it's precious. Of course, I would rather they experience joy, but it's precious just to be there with them and with whatever is alive in them. That's what my friend meant by "play with my pain." •

Staying Present in the Face of Strong Feelings

PARTICIPANT S: How do you stay really present and not get swept up in all these feelings?

MARSHALL: I don't know how to do that all the time. I was trying to do some healing work with a woman from Algeria who wanted some healing from me. Extremists had dragged her outside and made her watch while they tied her best friend behind a car and dragged this friend to her death. Then they took the woman inside and raped her in front of her parents. They were going to come back the next night and kill her, but she got to a phone and called friends of mine in Geneva who got her out in the middle of the night.

I got a phone call from them where I live in Switzerland. And they said, "Marshall, can you do the healing work with this woman?" They told me what had happened.

I said, "I'm doing a training during the day, but send her over this evening."

They said, "Marshall, here's the problem. We told her how you'll do the healing work, that you will play the role of the other person. She's afraid she'll kill you."

I said, "You explained this is role-play—it's not the actual person?"

They said, "She understands that. But she says, 'Even if I imagine he's that person, I'll kill him. I know I will.' And, Marshall, you should know that she's a large woman."

I thanked them for the warning, and then I said, "I'll tell you what. I'm going to have to have an interpreter in the room. It might make her feel safer to know that there's going to be another person there. I've got a guy in my training from Rwanda, and after what he's been through, I don't think this will scare him. Ask her if she will feel safe if this guy from Rwanda is in there to help me out if needed."

So those were the conditions under which she was there.

To address your question, when I started to hear this woman's pain, the enormity of her suffering, twice I just said, "Time out, time out. I need time." I had to go out into the hall and do a lot of work on myself to be able to go back. I couldn't just "go back" to her. The only thing I wanted to do at that point was to find those guys and do a little "Detroit therapy" with them. I had to work on myself for twenty minutes or so before I could go back to her.

What I'm saying, then, is that sometimes my pain is so great, I'm not able to be as fully present as I'd like. And I haven't found that to be a big problem. The other person can understand it usually.

PARTICIPANT S: Don't you think it's helpful sometimes to share that pain with the other person?

MARSHALL: Very often I do. I say to the other person, "I'm in such pain, I can't hear you right now. Do you want to hear what that pain is, or are you in too much pain yourself?" I'd say that half the time, the other person wants to hear it, and is able to. So that's another option. In this case though, she was crying so hard and screaming, and I wasn't at all optimistic that she needed to deal with my feelings. *

Empathy Steps

MARSHALL: Back to our empathy steps. *First,* empathy requires presence—a focus on what is alive in the other person at this moment, on that person's feelings and needs. *Second,* it requires checking things out with the other person, making sure you're connecting with that person's feelings and needs. Both steps we've mentioned so far can be done silently—by being fully present and having your attention on the other person's feelings and needs.

We can also check our understanding verbally, reflecting aloud what we sense the feelings and needs are. Let's remember to have our intention be to create empathy, as opposed to practicing a mechanical technique. The number one reason for checking aloud is to be sure we're connecting to others. We don't want them to see us as using something on them. So when we check it out, we do it in a way that lets others know we're not sure we're connecting fully and we'd like to verify what's real for them about what they've said.

The other condition under which we might check it out—even if we're pretty confident we've heard them—occurs when we sense that they really made themselves vulnerable in saying what they did. We can guess that, if we were in that position, we would really appreciate some confirmation that we were understood. These are the only two conditions under which we communicate empathy out loud instead of silently.

I was recently in Denmark working with a woman with an enormous amount of pain. At least twenty minutes had passed. She expressed her pain very beautifully, but she did it pretty nakedly. It was very easy for me to hear what was alive in her. I didn't feel any need to reflect it out loud; so for twenty minutes, I sat there silently. At the end of those twenty minutes, she just jumped up and hugged me and said, "Thank you for all of that empathy, Marshall." I had not said one word. I was with her the whole time. She felt it without a word being spoken.

PARTICIPANT R: So, with empathy, you're empty of yourself and full of the other person.

MARSHALL: With empathy, I'm fully *with* them, not full *of* them—that's sympathy.

The *third* step for empathizing is to stay with them until they give you signs that they're finished. Be aware that very often the first one or two messages that people give us are but the tip of the iceberg; we haven't gotten down to the bottom. There are a couple of signs to help us determine whether people are finished with empathy. One sign is the relief you can feel in them: empathy feels damn good. So if they got the empathy they need, you can feel that sense of relief, and you'll feel it in your own body. Anyone in the room with you will feel it. Another sign is they will often stop talking.

The *fourth* step doesn't happen until the relief is felt. During the empathy process, if every time I understand something and they come back with, "Yes, and blah, blah, blah, blah, blah, blah," that's a signal that they need more empathy. But when I feel this relief in tension, when I see that they have stopped talking, chances are they've received the empathy they needed. But I always like to triple-check by saying to them, "Is there more that you'd like to say?" I've learned to be very slow in shifting my attention away from them to myself, so it doesn't hurt to check again.

It would help if people we are doing the empathy work with knew how to say, "Finished," but most people don't. And most of the time, even after the empathy, they want something else. Our *fifth* step, then, is to empathize with their "postempathic" request, or that something extra they want. This request might be for information about how we feel having heard what they've said, especially if they've been very vulnerable.

It's a very human thing to want to know how what you've given has affected another person. Still, most people don't know how to ask for that. So if, after the empathy, I see them looking at me, I usually say, "Would you like to hear how I feel about what you said?" Sometimes they do, and sometimes they don't want to hear how I feel.

In addition to wanting information about how the person giving empathy feels, sometimes the postempathic request is for some kind of advice about better meeting their needs. When it comes to advising your child, however, never give advice unless you receive a request in writing first signed by a lawyer. Triple-check that your child wants advice, because it's almost always my first reaction to skip the empathy and go directly to the advice. •

THE FOUR STAGES OF HEALING

The First Stage of Healing: Empathy

We started with me playing the role of the other person—the brother—giving the sister empathy for her pain. Being with her, I sensed that she would like to get some verification, and I checked out loud most of the time. I tried to be fully present to her feelings and needs. But notice that I did all of this in the role of the brother. Why didn't I do it just as myself? As Marshall? I think that anyone giving her empathy would have helped to heal her. However, over the years, I've found that it's more powerful the closer the empathy comes to the real thing. In this example, if the brother were around, I would've wanted to help him give that empathy directly to his sister. But since she didn't have him here, I played the role of the brother.

To sum up, then, the first stage in the healing process is to give someone the empathy they need. There are three ways to do it: you can give it as a third party, you can play the role of the other person involved, or you can get that other person there to give it in person.

The Second Stage of Healing: Mourning in NVC

The second overall step in the healing process is mourning. In the role of the brother, after I empathized, I mourned. Here's what that sounded like: "Sister, when I see how my actions have contributed to your pain, I feel very sad. It didn't meet my need to nurture and support you in a way I really would've liked."

The main thing here is that it requires us to see a big difference between mourning and apology. I see apology as a very violent act. It is violent to the person receiving it and violent to the person giving it. What's even more tragic is that people receiving an apology usually like it—they are addicted by the culture to want the person apologizing to suffer and to see that person full of self-hate. What I find to be true is that people will never apologize or want an apology if they have experienced sincere mourning instead. Let's look at the difference between mourning and apology more closely.

Apology is based on moralistic judgment, that what I did was wrong and I should suffer for it—I should even hate myself for what I did. That's radically different from mourning, which is not based on moralistic judgments. Mourning is based on life-serving judgments. Did I meet my own needs? No. Then what need didn't I meet?

When we are in touch with our unmet need, we never feel shame, guilt, self-anger, or the depression that we feel when we think that what we did was wrong. We feel sadness, deep sadness, sometimes frustration, but never depression, guilt, anger, or shame. Those four feelings tell us we are making moralistic judgments at the moment we are feeling those feelings. Anger, depression, guilt, and shame are the product of the thinking that is at the base of violence on our planet. And I'm glad to have those feelings, because if I'm thinking in a way that I believe supports violence on our planet, I want as quickly as possible to transform that thinking.

In our second step, then, I mourned; I didn't apologize, I mourned.

Getting Unstuck

PARTICIPANT R: In your work, do you come across people who go into mourning and don't find a way to complete it?

MARSHALL: No, usually what keeps us stuck is moralistic thinking and judgments. I like the way Ernest Becker, the anthropologist, put it in his book *The Revolution in Psychiatry*. He agreed with Thomas Szasz, a psychiatrist, that "mental illness" is a tragic metaphor. Instead, he showed a different way of looking at the phenomenon.

Becker's definition of depression relates to your idea about getting stuck and never coming out of it: "Depression results from cognitively arrested alternatives." This means that our thinking blocks us from being aware of our needs and then being able to take action to meet our needs.

Let's take an example of someone mourning who is having trouble completing it. The person mourning thinks over and over, "I'm a poor parent. If I had treated my child differently, he wouldn't have run away from home and been killed on the train, running away from me. I should've known better. What's wrong with me? I'm a terrible parent." You get the idea. That kind of thinking can go on for years and years, and the person never gets out of it. But that's not mourning. That's getting stuck in moralistic thinking, all the "should haves." It doesn't go anywhere. "I'm a terrible person" is static thinking. That's what gets us stuck.

PARTICIPANT R: Could you repeat that quotation and explain a little more about it?

MARSHALL: "Depression results from cognitively arrested alternatives." Translated into my language, it's that our thinking keeps us from being aware of our needs, and taking steps to meet our needs. We get stuck in our thoughts.

I'll give another example. I work with very depressed people labeled as "bipolar" this and "depressive reaction" that. They sit there so depressed, thinking, "Oh, I don't want to live." If I use the empathic language of Nonviolent Communication and ask, "Could you tell me what needs of yours are not getting met?" I would get from them, "I'm a terrible failure." I'm asking their needs, but they're telling me what they, as people, are: "I'm a terrible friend."

We also get stuck if we compare ourselves to someone else: "My sister's two years younger than me, and she's an administrator in her business. Look at me. I'm only an assistant supervisor." I'm stuck by comparing. If you're comparing yourself to others, you must have read Dan Greenburg's book *How to Make Yourself Miserable*. One chapter teaches that if you don't know how to be depressed, just compare your-self to other people. And if you don't know how to do that, he's got some exercises. One shows a picture of a man and a woman who would be described as handsome and beautiful by contemporary standards. All of their measurements are on the picture. Greenburg's exercise is this: take your measurements, compare them to the measurements of these beautiful people, and think about the difference. Even if you start off happy, I guarantee that if you do that exercise, you will end up depressed. Greenburg doesn't stop there. Just when you think you are as depressed as you can get, you turn the page, and he says:

> Now, this is just a warm-up, because we all know that beauty is skin deep and that's not important. Let's now compare ourselves to people on dimensions that are important. Like what have you achieved in your stage of life with some other people that I have pulled at random from the phone book. I've interviewed these people and asked them what they've achieved, and now you can compare yourself.

The first person he gets out of the phone book is Mozart. I don't know a lot about history, but I don't think Mozart had a phone, so I don't entirely trust Greenburg here. But anyway, he says this man, Mozart, has written several pieces of music that have lasted over the centuries as masterpieces, *et cetera, et cetera.*

PARTICIPANT R: Started when he was five.

MARSHALL: Started when he was five. Now compare what you've achieved at your stage in life with what Mozart had achieved by age five. You can see that comparing yourself to others doesn't get you anywhere. That can go on forever; you never get out of it. That kind of thinking is taught in schools and supported by the manufacturers of antidepressants. The more you think that way, the more business for them is going to be good. •

The Third Stage of Healing: Acknowledgment of Past Needs

Let's briefly review the stages we've undertaken. First, Sister got empathy from me in the role of Brother. Second, I, the brother, mourned—not apologized, mourned—and that required a consciousness of my needs that weren't met. I also expressed the feelings that came with those needs not getting met. In the third stage of the healing process, Brother acknowledges to Sister what was going on in him when he did what he did. So playing the role of the brother, I said to her, "I'd really like to tell you what was going on in me at the time that I was doing that. I had these messages inside my head telling me I should help you, hearing them coming from outside of me. Understand, Sister, that I'm not saying you yourself said those messages, but I was hearing them inside me and as a demand. So I was torn inside: I wanted to help you, and at the same time, my need for autonomy was threatened by my hearing 'shoulds' inside and outside."

The Fourth Stage of Healing: Reverse Empathy

In the fourth stage, we turn the empathy around. In this final stage of the healing process—getting empathy for the person who did the act that stimulated the other person's pain—it's very important that it be done when the person in pain is ready to empathize. Almost always, people who have been in a lot of pain tell me that they've had somebody say, "You should empathize with the other person. If you empathize, you'll feel better about it." I think it's true that the healing is deep when we can empathize with what's going on in the person who raped us, who did something harmful to us. But to ask people to do that before they have had the empathy they need is just to commit further violence to them.

As a further example, let's go back to the woman I mentioned from Algeria and to the part of the process where I was going to role-play the other person, expressing what was going on in me (him) when I (he) violated her so terribly. Twice she screamed at me, "How could you have done it?" She was asking me, "How?" because there is a hunger in people to understand. But each time she said it, I could see she was still in too much pain to listen and then to give me empathy.

As I said, I take a lot of time getting to these last two stages of the healing process. I want to make sure others have had the empathy they need. So I say, "I will tell you how, but first I want to be sure that you have all the understanding you need." When that is finished, the woman—or any person—is usually hungry to empathize with me—that is, with the person who hurt them. •

PROCESS VERSUS MECHANICS

PARTICIPANT S: I was experimenting with NVC once with somebody else who was also practicing. What really upsets me is that when I am trying to do it, the other person also practicing empathy says, "Okay, you didn't express your feelings," or, "You didn't . . ." Maybe practicing has to be a little mechanical in the beginning, but can't the technique be more of a natural process? If I skip a step, I want to have freedom to do that. For example, you said that after empathy, you mourn. If I'm so structure-oriented that I think I need to do everything exactly literally, then if I don't feel like mourning, I will be fake with myself, which is exactly the opposite of what I think it is you're suggesting to be in contact with. I really have a need to remind myself that the technique is a great help, but that it won't work for me by itself without being true to what I'm feeling in that moment.

MARSHALL: I like very much what you're saying. It was said in a slightly different way by a woman in Zurich, Switzerland. She had come to a workshop and saw a husband and wife working with me; she saw what happened when they empathically connected with each other in a conflict that they'd had for a long time. She saw how beautiful it was to just see the energy in their faces when, for once, they weren't having enemy images and were really hearing each other. And it had been a very painful conflict, maybe fifteen years of going over it. The Swiss woman came back a year later and said, "You know, Marshall, in the year since I was in your workshop, every time I'm in a difficult situation, I bring to my consciousness the look on the woman's and man's faces when they connected empathically." And then she said, "Then, even when I speak in a hurtful or harming way, it's still NVC." You see, she had it the way you do now. The mechanics are only helpful to the degree to which they support our connecting in a certain way. If we get so preoccupied with the mechanics that they become the only objective, we've lost the process.

Now, this is one of the hardest things about our training, because one of the things that people say they like about our training is that it really helps them manifest in concrete ways what they've always believed. So they like the fact that it is a way of concretely manifesting. However, its very concreteness can be a disadvantage when it becomes an objective to do it right.

SLOWING DOWN AND TAKING TIME

PARTICIPANT R: I'm working and struggling in my life with this whole issue of slowing my body down, slowing my relationships down, so I can be more present to myself and to other people and to life. I see you doing this constant traveling. I would find it inspiring and helpful to hear if it's true that you weren't always this slow and to learn a little bit about the evolution of how you slowed yourself down.

MARSHALL: I think it's related to what Participant S was saying. In the middle of the rat race, it's very important for me to know how to choose to make use of the three words I probably have said to myself more than any three words in the past forty years: *take your time.* Those three words give you the power to come from a spirituality of your own choosing, not the one you were programmed for.

In my meditation materials, I have a very powerful picture that helps me remember to take my time. A friend of mine from Israel is very active in organizing Israelis and Palestinians who've lost children in the struggle and who want to create something else out of the misery. So one of the steps was to write a book in honor of his son who had been killed; he used the energy that he suffered from to go in a different direction. He gave me a copy of the book. And even though it was written in Hebrew and I couldn't read it, I am glad he did, because I opened it up, and there on the first page is the last picture taken of his son before he was killed in the battle of Lebanon. On the son's T-shirt it says, "Take Your Time." I asked my friend, the author/father, if he had a bigger-sized picture that I could have to help me remember. I told him why those three words were so important to me. He said, "Then let me tell you also, Marshall, this will probably make it even more powerful. When I went to my son's commanding officer to ask, 'Why did you send him? Couldn't you see that anybody you asked to do that was going to get killed?' he said, 'We didn't take our time.' That's why I put that picture in there of my son."

It's critical for me to be able to slow down, take my time, to come from an energy I choose, the one I believe that we were meant to come from, not the one I was programmed into.

My Israeli friend also said, "Marshall, I'll give you a poem written by an Israeli poet who was influenced the same way you were when he saw the picture." And the first line in his poem is, "Take your time, it's yours you know." And I have to keep working at that because, as my beloved partner keeps pointing out, I forget it, and I start to race.

EMPATHY FOR THOSE WHO WOULD HURT YOU

PARTICIPANT R: I've heard you say that children are less likely to be beaten by someone if they empathize with the person ready to beat them. I assume this applies to adults as well. Do you have any suggestions or emergency phrases that they might pull out at that time?

MARSHALL: Yes. The first thing we teach them is never to put your "but" in your dad's face when he's angry. So, when Daddy says, "Why did you do this?" don't reply, "But Dad. . . ." Never give an explanation.

What to do instead is, as fast as you can, put your attention on what your dad is feeling and needing. Be conscious that he's not angry at you; you didn't make him angry. But hear his anger and hear what need isn't getting met.

We practice, practice, practice this. It's one thing to talk about it theoretically, but it's another thing, when someone's about to beat you, to know how to empathically connect with what's alive in that person. We teach police how to do this in dangerous conditions. A lot of research has documented that police are far more likely to come out alive when dealing with violent people if the police officers are armed with empathy rather than with a gun.

But to ask kids to do it is a bigger challenge. So we have to give children a great deal of practice. If you're around parents who think that they always know what's right and that if people are wrong they should be punished for it, then it's likely that you will beat your own child as well. Until we can get hold of the parents the child lives with, we teach the children the best self-defense we know: empathic connection.

DEALING WITH YOUR OWN ANGRY BEHAVIOR

PARTICIPANT S: How do you deal with your own personal violent behavior when you've communicated with another person and gone through everything, and you get to the point where you feel like blowing up? When the traffic's bad, when you're going to the airport, or whatever?

MARSHALL: If you follow me around when I leave here this evening, you will probably see twenty such situations between now and when I get to Santa Barbara tonight. My partner's sleeping now—otherwise, she would verify that.

PARTICIPANT S: And you go through that whole process of mentally calming yourself down and doing all that?

MARSHALL: Yes. So now I suffer for about thirty seconds instead of about three hours. But I still get triggered. You see, there is this horrible breed of violent, evil people called "people who don't move fast enough." When I want to get through the ticket line, and I want to sit down and just relax, this breed of people—these jerks—are all over the damn planet, and they're placed here to aggravate the hell out of me. There's an international plot to test my patience in my Nonviolent Communication.

PARTICIPANT S: So do you have a trick or a special trigger that you've come up with? Do you count to ten or something?

MARSHALL: No, my anger is valuable. It's really a blessing. When I'm angry, I know I need to slow down and look at what I'm telling myself—I need to translate the judgments that are making me angry and get in touch with my needs.

PARTICIPANT S: So you believe anger is justified in certain situations?

MARSHALL: Anger is always justified in the sense that it's the inevitable result of life-alienated, violence-provocative thinking. Anger is not the problem. It's the thinking that's going on in us when we're angry that's the problem.

PARTICIPANT S: And what is the process that you use to deal with it?

MARSHALL: I slow down, and I enjoy the judgment show going on in my head. I don't tell myself I "shouldn't" think that way. That's perpetuating it. I don't say it's wrong. I don't say to myself what my son once asked me, when I said these judgmental thoughts out loud: "You go around the world teaching communication?" I try not to say to myself, "I don't think it's justified." I just see it, connect with the need behind it, and give empathy to myself. I hear the need behind this moralistic thinking.

As an example, I might be frustrated because I'd like the line to go faster, but in the ten minutes that I'm going to be in that line, I'm not going to be putting additional stress on my heart. (By the way, research in the medical arena shows a high correlation between "Type A" thinking, which is what I call moralistic or judgmental thinking, and heart disease.) So I'd like to slow down the stress on my heart to about thirty beats a second, rather than being in that line for ten minutes, angry at the person up front who's taking up all this time talking to the ticket seller. "Don't they know I'm back here?" I can let this stress eat at my heart, or I can choose to really transform that frustration. If I slow down, I can ask myself what could I do in those ten minutes? I could carry something to read in the line.

PARTICIPANT S: Is the ultimate goal to not be perturbed by it at all? Is that where you see yourself eventually?

MARSHALL: The ultimate goal is to spend as many of my moments in life as I can in that world that the poet Rumi talks about, "a place beyond rightness and wrongness."

LEARNING TO DEAL WITH A DIFFICULT PERSON

PARTICIPANT S: Aside from right and wrong, I think we all have our conditioning, a certain chemistry and openness toward some people and not toward others, based on our upbringing, personal habits, and all. I often don't know how to genuinely feel open and warm to people who are different, really different, from me. And I'm not necessarily just talking about racism. It might just be people with different habits, different ways of going about things, and so I'm confused about how to genuinely develop more tolerance. It's more difficult in this politically correct society that says we should be tolerant.

MARSHALL: First, get the word *should* out of there. As long as I think I "should" do it, I'll resist it, even if I want very much to do it. Hearing "should" from inside or outside takes all the joy out of doing it. I try to never do anything I should do. Instead, I follow Joseph Campbell's suggestion. After studying comparative religion and mythology for forty-three years, Campbell said, "You know, after all of my research, it's amazing that all religions are saying the same thing: don't do anything that isn't playful." Don't do anything that isn't play. He also said it another way: "Follow your bliss." Come from this energy of how to make the world fun and learnable.

Let's talk for a minute about "tolerance." There are a lot of people I can't stand being around, and they are my best gurus. They teach me about what's going on in me that makes it hard to see the divine energy in them. I want to learn from anything that keeps me from connecting to that energy. Fortunately, there are a lot of people I can't stand; I have a lot of learning opportunities. I practice. I ask, "What do these people do that is a trigger for my judging them?" First, I try to get clear about what they do, and, second, I try to be conscious about how I'm judging those who make me so angry. The third step is to look behind my judgment to see what particular need of mine is not getting met in relation to those people. I try to give myself empathy for what need of mine isn't met in relation to them. Fourth, I say to myself, "When people do that thing that I don't like, what personal need are they trying to meet?" I try to empathize with what's alive in them when they do it.

These people whom I can't stand are my best teachers of Nonviolent Communication if I do that exercise with them.

ANGER TOWARD MOTHERS

PARTICIPANT S: I would like to know if you would be willing to help me with some healing with my mother? I'm going to be visiting her for Thanksgiving.

MARSHALL: Let's do it. I'll be your mother, and you play yourself.

MARSHALL, AS MOTHER: Well, son, I've got my empathy ears on now, and I would like very much to hear anything that's alive in you that makes it less than totally enjoyable for you to be around me.

PARTICIPANT S: Where do I begin?

MARSHALL, AS MOTHER: Oh, good, there's a lot I can learn.

PARTICIPANT S: I'm so frustrated and angry and discouraged, and I feel despair around how negative you are, how you're always looking at things to criticize about the world, about me, about life, about the government. I'm angry that you painted this picture that the world is a horrible place and then said it to me and to my sisters.

MARSHALL, AS MOTHER: Let me see if I can get that. I hear two important messages in there that I don't want to miss. First, if I'm hearing you correctly, you'd like some understanding about how painful it is for you to be around me when I'm in so much pain and how it leaves you constantly feeling under some pressure to have some way to deal with my pain.

PARTICIPANT S: Yes.

MARSHALL, AS MOTHER: And the second thing I'm hearing that you'd like from me is some understanding of how much pain you carry with you from having been exposed to this for so long, that you'd like not to have so much pain in how you see things.

PARTICIPANT S: That's partly accurate. I'm angry because it feels like I have to fight inside of myself, to protect my own ability to choose, to perceive things the way I want.

MARSHALL, AS MOTHER: So how wonderful it would be if you didn't have to work so hard to live in a world that is quite different from the one that I painted for you.

PARTICIPANT S: Yeah.

MARSHALL, AS MOTHER: Yeah. How much you'd like to live in that other world and how sad it is to see how much of your energy goes into the one that I helped you learn to live in.

PARTICIPANT S: Yeah, and this sounds blaming—and it is—but that's where I am right now.

MARSHALL, AS MOTHER: I can't hear blame, son. I have my NVC ears on. All I can hear is beauty.

PARTICIPANT S: I'm angry that you're just in so much pain that that's all you present, and that you didn't say, "I'm in a lot of pain, but you don't have to be." And I'm angry that I wasn't given any encouragement to choose a different way of looking at the world, and when I do present a different way, you feel threatened, and you try to devalue and diminish what I perceive.

MARSHALL, AS MOTHER: I want to reflect that, to check with you to see whether it could have at least made things more bearable for you, if while I was in this pain, I could've said, "Hey, this is just how I look at it, and I'm not encouraging you to see it this way." But instead I presented it in a way that sounded like this is the way the world is, and as a child you internalized that. And that is now what makes it so hard for you to live in the world of your choosing, rather than the one I painted for you.

PARTICIPANT S: Yes. And I go into that child place a lot when I'm with you. I don't have the distance that I feel like I need to be able to say, "Ah, that's just my mom." It still feels like it threatens my autonomy to hear your feelings.

MARSHALL, AS MOTHER: Yeah, you hear those feelings, and you lose connection with the world you want to be in, and you go into this world that I painted for you.

PARTICIPANT S: Yeah. And I'm worried because I'm going to visit you on Thanksgiving, and I know a lot of the strategies that I've used in the past are still alive in me, like nodding my head up and down, pretending to listen when I'm really angry and I've actually left my body. I'm too scared to express my real feelings, and I'm worried that I'm going to do that again. And I'm worried that if I do try to be authentic with you, that I'm going to be criticized for having these feelings.

MARSHALL, AS MOTHER: You hate to be in this situation, where the only two options you can imagine are hiding yourself or trying to be honest and making a bigger mess. You'd really like there to be some other connection between us besides that.

PARTICIPANT S: Yeah. And I'm worried about the part of me that is so hurt about this that I want to shame you and make you wrong.

MARSHALL, AS MOTHER: How you suffered is so strong in you that you desperately need this understanding of how much you've paid for this.

PARTICIPANT S: Yeah. Yeah. Being authentic and making a mess isn't the thing that scares me the most though, because I have some training in being able to clean it up. What I hate about myself is that I can freeze up and just not be there. And not take care of myself and not speak up. I'm worried about that tendency.

MARSHALL, AS MOTHER: So, as uncomfortable as it is for you to imagine speaking up and having to clean up the mess, that's less toxic for you than continuing to hide yourself and not express yourself—as scary as it is to do that.

PARTICIPANT S: I have a lot of pain about internalizing the labels "too sensitive" and "hypersensitive"—the labels that you use to express your being overwhelmed when you hear my feelings.

MARSHALL, AS MOTHER: Yeah, yeah, yeah. You wish you could hear through that and hear my pain without hearing any criticism, but it's a real strain for you to do that.

PARTICIPANT S: Yeah.

MARSHALL, AS MOTHER: Is there more you'd like me to hear before I respond?

PARTICIPANT S: I'm really worried about how much pain is still alive in me and how that comes out as me wanting to make you wrong, wanting to shame you and beat you up for what I perceive you did to me.

MARSHALL, AS MOTHER: Yeah, the pain is so strong in you, and you need to get it out. But you're afraid that the only way it might come out is going to be interpreted by me in a way that will make both of us even more distant from one another. And that's not what you want. But you do want to be able to get that pain out and dealt with.

PARTICIPANT S: Yeah, I'm worried about intellectualizing. I wish I had the permission, the psychic permission, to just scream and stamp my feet and not say any words. I'd like to have that heard, because we get into our heads, and I hate that.

MARSHALL, AS MOTHER: Yeah. So, you want to be sure that if we do use words, that they really connect us to life and not take us farther from it. And at the moment, it's hard to imagine any words that would do that. It seems like to get all the pain out, you just have to scream or stomp or something.

PARTICIPANT S: And I'm also connected to a part of me that just wants to come home and get the nurturing that I did not get as a child in this family, and I'm worried that that's not a very realistic need to try to get met in this family.

MARSHALL, AS MOTHER: So there's more than just resolving all this pain. You really have a dream of a nurturing relationship, of feeling you're valued, of enjoying our being with one another. That seems so far off, given all the pain that you're going through, that it's hard to even imagine we could get to that stage of really being nurturing for one another.

PARTICIPANT S: Uh-huh. To be honest, it's hard to imagine you ever giving that, because you're so caught up in your own suffering.

MARSHALL, AS MOTHER: Yeah. So hard to even imagine. Is there anything more you want me to hear before I respond?

PARTICIPANT S: You know, if you talk about how much you hate the president, even if I agree with you, I don't want to hear it, and I'd rather punch you in the face.

MARSHALL, AS MOTHER: So, whatever I'm talking about, whether it's the president or something else, as soon as you see me in pain, you get yourself in such pain that it's not a place you want to continue to be in.

PARTICIPANT S: I don't have any idea why, intellectually, but just hearing you vent your judgments about people pisses me off. I don't want to be a sounding board for your storytelling. If I saw you releasing your pain and getting empathy for that, it would be a different story, but . . .

MARSHALL, AS MOTHER: You're fed up with feeling that somehow you have to heal that pain, but not knowing how to do it and getting yourself down. You want something else out of any relationship you're in, besides being in that role. You're tired of having to listen to it and then somehow make me feel better.

PARTICIPANT S: Uh-huh. I wish I could find a way to enjoy it. You know? Hearing your judgments versus the way I hear a friend's judgments. You and I sometimes have a party hurting one another. And I'm not there, because I have this critical voice inside telling me it's my responsibility.

MARSHALL, AS MOTHER: You're aware that part of the issue is telling yourself that somehow you need to fix me, your mom. But also you want me to see that there are things that I say and do that provoke that.

PARTICIPANT S: Yeah, it would feel really nice for me if you said, "You know, I've got some pain, and I'd like to vent. Can I have an ear?" To actually ask for permission. Then I could get my needs met for respect.

MARSHALL, AS MOTHER: Yeah. I'd like to respond now. Can you hear me, or would you like me to hear more of you?

PARTICIPANT S: I can say a lot more, but I feel okay about hearing you now.

MARSHALL, AS MOTHER: Well, I'm so relieved that you haven't given up on our relationship, that you still are working at finding a way to make it not only bearable but also nurturing. And I'm sure you've been close to giving up on it. I can't tell you what a gift it is—that despite the pain you're telling me about, you're still looking for hope, some glimmer that we can learn to nurture one another.

PARTICIPANT S: I don't know that I have that hope, but I know that if I work on this a little bit, I'll have better relationships with women.

MARSHALL, AS MOTHER: So even if you can't imagine getting nurture from me, you would hope at least that you could with other women.

There's so much I want to tell you that's stimulated in me by what you've said, but, at the moment, there's just a horrible sadness to see that I handled my pain in a way that didn't meet one of the needs that I've had my whole life, the strongest need that I can think of: to nurture you. And to see that instead of nurturing you in a way that I would've liked, I've been a stimulus for so much pain for you. It's enormously frightening to look at my depth of sadness about that. It's one thing that I had to suffer myself, but to have contributed to all this pain in you, that's a really, really painful sadness to look at. And I'd like to know how you feel when you hear me say that.

PARTICIPANT S: I feel kind of numb. I think I'm protecting myself.

MARSHALL, AS MOTHER: That's what I was afraid of, that even now you feel that you have to do something about it. I really do want you to know that, with these ears on, all I want is empathy. Nothing else. And if you can't give it, I can hear that without hearing it as a rejection or creating more pain.

So I can hear that you're kind of numb and part of you wants to resonate to it, but part of you is afraid of getting into the old now-you-have-to-do-something-about-it.

Now, I'd like to tell you what goes on in me when I've been acting the way I have over the years. When I hear how you would've liked for me to have said it, really I want to cry because it makes me aware that I would've liked to have said it in that way. Then I ask myself what kept me from doing it, and that's when I want to cry. I can't even imagine that anyone really cares about what's going on for me. And then what you said helped me realize that I've been asking for it in a way that leads to self-fulfilling prophecies. The way I've been asking for it, how can anybody enjoy giving it to me? And I just felt such a depth of sadness that I didn't know other ways of saying, "Hey, I'm in pain, and I need some attention."

I don't want you to take responsibility for my pain. I just need somehow to feel that somebody cares about what's going on for me. The only way I knew to ask for that provoked just the opposite from almost everybody, going back to the time I was a child. I never had the feeling that my needs mattered to somebody. Therefore, to ask for it in a way the other person might enjoy hearing it wasn't a possibility. I just get desperate and express it in the only way I know how: out of desperation. And then I see how it affects other people, and I get even more desperate.

I'd like to know how you feel when I tell you that.

PARTICIPANT S: Sad, but somewhat relieved to be able to hear some of what was behind the urgency of your expression. I feel some relief in just connecting with it.

MARSHALL, AS MOTHER: I'm feeling very vulnerable about our revelation of ourselves. How would you feel if I asked the group for their reaction to what we've been saying?

PARTICIPANT S: I'd probably enjoy that.

MARSHALL, AS HIMSELF: Okay, does anybody have any feelings or reactions to our dialogue?

Reactions to the Role-Play

PARTICIPANT R: Somehow, it just makes my heart smile to see men being so responsive in such a compassionate way. This is a new kind of experience for me.

MARSHALL: [Jokingly.] We're not *real* men.

PARTICIPANT R: Your modeling it for me opens up a possibility for a way for men to act. So I'm grateful.

PARTICIPANT T: I, too, am grateful. It really touched my heart deeply, because my mother and I have a similar dynamic, one that I've not found an effective way to deal with. I've just kind of gone to a place of hopelessness about it. As I was listening to Marshall mourn in the mother role, with the sadness over how her intention was for her son to be happy and how important that was to her, I felt some healing for me, knowing that's what's important to my mother—that it was never her intention to make my life hard. It was healing for me to hear what she may have been going through and to hear your dialogue. I really appreciate that.

PARTICIPANT U: Well, I feel very grateful for the experience, because I could really sense the humanity behind the words.

I don't know if anybody's heard about "vibrations," but I felt something at one point that took away the separateness between me and each person in this room. I felt really connected. And on the other side, I'm a little sad, because I really would like to see people—myself included—happy, you know? And I'm realizing what you were saying when you were role-playing the mother: that there is something that blocks the humanity in each one of us, and it's amazing how quickly a solution can happen once one or maybe both persons are able to open up. I think the technique helps a lot, but it's also about your ability to connect with your heart; it's about the presence I felt. Like believing in God. I think that's a good description of what I felt in the moment. Thank you very much.

PARTICIPANT S: What's alive in me is my sadness, identifying with you, recognizing that I've given up on healing my relationship with my own mother . . . how I was just going to heal my relationship with women without having to heal with my mother. And how I don't know how to approach her, or even if I can or should, because I don't think she could really respond like that to me.

MARSHALL: How do you think she would respond upon hearing this recording?

PARTICIPANT S: I don't know. It has been healing for me; maybe it would heal her or something.

MARSHALL: I'd like you to try it, and if it works beautifully I'd like you to call me and tell me. And if it messes things up, call my staff.

PARTICIPANT R: I also feel some hope after hearing that—not that I could stay with feelings and needs the whole time by any means, but I just feel some hope. Even if I screw it up, there's some hope and energy to try with my own brother, the same kind of thing. Thank you.

MARSHALL'S MOTHER'S GIFT TO HIM

MARSHALL: I'd like to share with you a gift I received. I had very similar pain in relationship to my mother, and you were speaking like it was me. I want to tell you about some major surgery that I had that helped me get out of it—not surgery done on me, but that my mother had at a workshop of mine that she attended.

In the workshop, women in the group were talking about how scary it was for them as women to express needs directly and how much their personal relationships with men were getting all mucked up because of it. The only way they knew how to express needs got the opposite of what they wanted. Then they got more bitter, which made it worse.

One woman after another was saying how hard it was for her to express her need. My mother got up and went to the bathroom. I started to worry because she was in there a really long time. When she came out, I noticed how pale she was, and I asked, "Mother, are you all right?" She said, "Now I am. It was very upsetting for me to hear the discussion, because when I heard the women talking about how hard it was for them to express their needs, it reminded me of something." I said, "Do you mind telling me what it was, Mother?"

She told me this story: "When I was fourteen, my sister, your aunt Minnie, had her appendix taken out. Your aunt Alice bought her a little purse. How I cherished that purse, what I wouldn't have given for that purse, but in our family you never asked for what you wanted or needed. If you did, you would hear back from one of the older kids, 'You know how poor we are. Why are you asking for what you need?' But I wanted it so badly that I started to complain of pains in my side. They took me to two doctors who couldn't find anything, but the third one said maybe we should do exploratory surgery."

They took out my mother's appendix. And it worked: my aunt Alice bought her a purse just like the one that my mother wanted but couldn't ask for.

But that wasn't the end of it. Mother told me, "I was lying in bed in the hospital in a lot of pain, but I was so happy. The nurse came in and stuck a thermometer in my mouth and then went out. Then another nurse came in. I wanted her to see my purse, but I could only say 'Mmmm, mmmm, mmmm' because of the thing in my mouth. The nurse said, 'For me? Thank you,' and she took the purse. And I couldn't ask for it back."

That was such a gift that my mother gave me, because just seeing how hard it was for her to express her needs, what she would go through, helped me see everything I hated her for. I understood that when she asked for the things that just aggravated the hell out of me, there was desperation behind it. I could see why she couldn't just come out and say it. So that major surgery helped shake me out of that. That really helped. •

PARTICIPANT T: Participant S, I really appreciate your willingness to be vulnerable and to express all your anger and your hurt and your pain. You may be surprised that your mother may be willing and anxious to open that up. I'm going to buy the recording and take it to my son.

PARTICIPANT S, TO MARSHALL: Could you say a few things that would bring some closure to my dialogue with you? I'm thinking about getting the recording and playing it for my mother when I visit her, and that idea brings up a lot of fear. What I'm telling myself is, we said some pretty strong, harsh things in the dialogue, and although I don't have any hope that I can have a better relationship with my mom, I'm worried that she might not be able to hear that as me just venting in the moment.

MARSHALL: That's the danger. But if she stays with it long enough and sees how I heard the beauty behind it, she'll also be learning Nonviolent Communication.

PARTICIPANT S: I just realized that before playing the recording, I can explain to her that some of the things I said were said just for the purpose of expressing the really strong emotion in the moment. She understands that very well. She taught me that.

MARSHALL: And then you can say, "And Mother, I'd like you to see how Marshall handled it in your role. And I'd like you to tell me afterward how you felt about how he played your role. How he dealt with it when I called you these names."

PARTICIPANT S: I'm worried she might want you for a son.

PARTICIPANT R: I want Marshall for a mother. '

SUMMARY

There are *four primary stages* in creating a bridge of empathy between people seeking healing or reconciliation in a significant relationship.

Stage One: Empathic Connection

1. **Being present:** I extend empathy to a person who is hurting, angry, or frightened by being fully present to what is alive in that person, without offering any judgment, diagnosis, or advice.
2. **Connecting with and checking out current feelings and needs:** I do so out loud *only if:*
   - my intention is to verify that I have accurately understood and connected with the person, and

- I sense that the person shared vulnerably and may appreciate verbal empathy from me. My focus is on what is alive in that person right now (as a result of what happened in the past) rather than on the story and past events.

3. **Staying in empathy:** I stay with the person until I receive visible signs that the person is finished (e.g., a sense of relief or a quieting down).

4. **Checking in:** I ask, "Is there more you'd like to say?"

5. **Receive postempathic request:** What would the person like from me in this moment? (Information? Advice? To know how I feel after having heard them speak?)

Remember to distinguish between empathy and sympathy. With empathy, I am fully present with others while *they* are feeling their feelings. With sympathy, I am back home feeling my own feelings.

Stage Two: Mourning

Mourning in NVC requires becoming conscious of my current unmet needs as a result of specific choices I made in the past. For example, in the role-play between the brother and sister, the brother says: "Sister, when I see how my actions have contributed to your pain, I feel very sad. It didn't meet my need to nurture and support you in a way I really would've liked." As he mourns, the brother also connects with the feeling that now arises (sadness) from those unmet needs (to nurture and support the sister).

NVC mourning is not apologizing. Apologies are based on moralistic judgments involving admission of wrongdoing and the implication that some form of suffering will "make it right." In NVC mourning, I ask myself whether my action met my needs. If not, I ask myself which needs I didn't meet and how I am feeling about it.

Stage Three: Acknowledgment of Past Needs
(That Led Me to Behave as I Did)

Following the stages of empathic connection and mourning, the earnest question I may hear asked of me is, "But why did you do it?" I make certain that the person has received all the empathy needed before moving to this next stage, where I address the question by connecting with the needs that I was trying to meet when I behaved as I had.

For example, in the mother–son role-play, after the mother empathized with the son and then mourned in his presence, she acknowledged what had led her to behave toward her family the way she had: "I never had the feeling that my needs mattered to somebody. I just got desperate and expressed it in the only way I knew how: out of desperation. And then I saw how it affected other people, and I got even more desperate. I just felt such a depth of sadness that I didn't know other ways of saying, 'Hey, I'm in pain, and I need some attention.'"

Just as mourning is distinct from apologizing, the mother's compassionate self-forgiveness based on connecting to her past feelings (desperation, pain) and needs (for caring attention and "to matter") is distinct from rationalization or denial of responsibility.

Stage Four: Reverse Empathy

After the person in pain has received full empathy, has heard my mourning, and has understood the needs I was trying to meet through my behavior, that person will feel a natural desire to turn around and empathize with me. When this happens, we will have completed the final stage of healing. It is critical, however, that this occurs only when there is a genuine urge on the other person's part to empathize with me. Any sense of pressure or a premature invitation will simply contribute to furthering that person's pain.

Editor's note: In the transcribed workshop used for this chapter, Marshall makes reference to, but does not demonstrate through role-plays, this final stage of healing.

4

The Surprising Purpose of Anger

Beyond Anger Management—
Finding the Gift

I n this chapter, I would like to share my perspective on the role anger can play in our lives. I hope to challenge you to shift away from the idea that anger is something to be suppressed. Instead, anger is a gift, challenging us to connect to the unmet needs that have triggered this reaction. I reveal common misconceptions about anger and how our anger is the product of thinking. A discussion of anger easily supports a better understanding of NVC, because it touches on so many key NVC distinctions. Living from your heart, making judgment-free observations, getting clear about your feelings and needs, making clear requests, and supporting life-enriching connections all relate to how you respond to anger.

ANGER AND NVC

When it comes to managing anger, NVC shows how to use anger as an alarm that tells us we are thinking in ways that are not likely to get our needs met and are more likely to get us involved in interactions that are not going to be very constructive for anyone. NVC training stresses that *it is dangerous to think of anger as something to be repressed or as something bad.* When we identify anger as a result of something wrong with us, our tendency is to want to repress it and not deal with it. That use of anger—to repress and deny it—often leads us to express it in ways that can be very dangerous to ourselves and others.

Think of how many times you've read in the newspapers about serial killers and how people who knew them described them. A rather typical description is, "He was always such a nice person. I never heard him raise his voice. He never seemed to be angry at anyone." In NVC, we are interested in using anger to help us get at the needs that are not being fulfilled within ourselves, that are at the root of our anger.

Many of the groups I work with around the world have witnessed the consequences of teaching that anger is something to be repressed. These groups have seen that when people are taught that anger should be avoided, it can be used to oppress them by getting them to tolerate whatever is happening. However, I also have reservations about how, in response to that concern, some have advocated cultivating or "venting" anger without understanding its roots and transforming it. Some studies have indicated that anger-management programs that simply encourage participants to vent anger—by, for example, beating pillows—just push the anger closer to the surface and, in fact, leave the participants more susceptible to expressing their anger later in ways that are dangerous to themselves and others.

What we want to do as we use NVC to manage anger is to go more deeply into it, to see what is going on within us when we are angry, to be able to get at the need—which is the root of anger—and then fulfill that need. For teaching purposes, I sometimes refer to anger as being similar to the warning light on the dashboard of a car—it's providing useful information about what the engine needs. You wouldn't want to hide or disconnect or ignore it. You'd want to slow down the car and figure out what the light's trying to tell you.

It Works Even If Only One Person Applies It

It has been my experience that if I can keep my attention on anger as a warning, no matter how the other person is communicating, then we both remain connected. In other words, NVC works even if only one person applies it.

It's not too hard to keep the focus in this direction. However, it can be scary, because it always requires vulnerability on our part to nakedly say how we are and what we would like. The process can flow fairly well when both parties are trained in it, but almost everyone I work with is attempting to establish this flow of communication with someone who is not likely to ever come to NVC workshops. So it's very important that this process work with anyone, whether or not they have been trained to communicate this way.

One thing we stress in our intensive training is how to stay with this process, regardless of how other people communicate. In one sense, anger is a fun way to dive more deeply into NVC, even if you are starting with this process for the first time. When you're angry, it brings many aspects of the NVC process into sharp focus, helping you see the difference between NVC and other forms of communication.

The NVC approach to anger involves several steps. I will go over these steps by using an example of a young man in a prison in Sweden. I was working with this man in a prisoner training session, showing the participants how NVC can be used to manage anger.

FOUR STEPS TO HANDLING ANGER

The First Step

The first step in handling anger using NVC is to be conscious that *the stimulus, or trigger, of the anger is not the cause of the anger.* In other words, it isn't simply what people do that makes us angry, it's actually something within us that responds to what they do—that is really the cause of the anger. This step requires us to be able to separate the trigger from the cause.

In the situation with the prisoner, the very day that we were focusing on anger, he had a lot of anger in relationship to the prison authorities. So he was very glad to have us there to help him deal with his anger.

I asked him what the prison authorities had done that was the stimulus of his anger. He answered, "I made a request of them three weeks ago, and they still haven't responded." He had answered the question in the way that I wanted him to. He had simply told me what they had *done.* He hadn't mixed in any evaluation, and that is the first step in managing anger in a nonviolent way: simply be clear about what the stimulus is, but don't mix that up with judgments or evaluation. This alone is an important accomplishment. Frequently when I ask such a question, I get a response such as, "They were inconsiderate," which is a moral judgment of what they "are" but that doesn't say what they actually did.

The Second Step

The second step involves being conscious that the stimulus is never the cause of anger. That is, it isn't simply what people do that makes us angry. *It is our evaluation of what has been done that is the cause of our anger.* This is a particular kind of evaluation. NVC is built on the premise that anger is the result of life-alienated ways of evaluating what is happening to us. It isn't directly connected to what we need or what the people around us need. Instead, it is based on ways of thinking that imply wrongness or badness on the part of others for what they have done.

Evaluating Triggers that Lead to Anger

There are four ways to evaluate any anger triggers that occur in our lives. In the case of the prison officials not responding for three weeks to his request, the prisoner could have looked at the situation and taken it personally, as a rejection. Had he done that, he would not have been angry. He might have felt hurt, he might have felt discouraged, but he wouldn't have felt angry.

As a second possibility, he could have looked within himself and seen what his needs were. Focusing directly on needs is a way of thinking that is most likely to get them met. As we will see later, had he been focused directly on his needs, he would not have been angry. He might have felt scared, which it turned out he was once he got in touch with his needs.

A third possibility is that he could have looked at things in terms of what needs the prison officials were experiencing that led them to behave as they did. This kind of understanding of the needs of others does not leave us feeling angry. In fact, when we are really directly connected with the needs of others—at the point at which we understand their needs—we are not really in touch with any feelings within ourselves, because our full attention is on the needs of others.

The fourth way he could have looked at things—which we will find is always at the base of anger—is to think in terms of the wrongness of the prison officials for behaving as they did. In NVC, whenever we feel angry, we say to ourselves, "I'm feeling angry because I am telling myself _____," and then we look for the kind of life-alienated thinking going on inside our head that is the cause of our anger.

In the case of the prisoner, when he told me he was angry and the trigger for his anger was that the prison officials hadn't responded for three weeks to his request, I asked him to look inside and tell me what the cause of his anger was. He seemed confused and said to me, "I just told you the cause of my anger. I made a request three weeks ago, and the prison officials still haven't responded to it."

I told him, "What you have told me is the trigger for your anger. In our previous sessions, I tried to clarify that it's never simply the trigger that creates our anger. The cause is what we're looking for. So I'd like you to tell me how you are interpreting their behavior—how you are looking at it—that is causing you to be angry."

He was very confused at this point. Like many of us, he had not been trained to be conscious of what was going on within himself when he was angry. So I had to give him a little help to give him an idea of what I meant by just stopping and listening to the thoughts that might be going on inside of his head and that are always at the core of anger.

After a few moments, he said to me, "OK, I see what you mean. I'm angry because I'm telling myself it isn't fair, that it isn't a decent way to treat human beings. They are acting as though they are important, and I'm nothing." He had several other such judgments floating rapidly through his head. Notice he initially said it was simply their behavior that was making him angry, when, in fact, it was really all these thoughts that he had within himself that were making him angry, any one of which could have created his anger. And he had been ready with a whole series of such judgments: "They're not fair; they're not treating me right." All such judgments are the cause of anger.

Once we had identified this, he said to me, "Well, what's wrong with thinking that way?"

I replied, "I'm not saying there's anything wrong with thinking that way. I'd just like you to be conscious that thinking that way is the cause of your anger. And we don't want to mix up what people do—the trigger—with the cause of anger."

Trigger Versus Cause

This idea can be very hard to keep straight: to not mix up the trigger, or stimulus, of anger with the cause of anger. The reason that it's not easy is that many of us were educated by people who use guilt as a primary form of motivation. If you want to use guilt to manipulate people, you first need to confuse them into thinking that the trigger is the cause of the feeling. In other words, if you want to use guilt with somebody, you need to communicate in a way that indicates that your pain is being caused simply by what they do. This means that their behavior is not simply the stimulus of your feelings, but it's also the cause of your feelings.

If you are a guilt-inducing parent, you might say to a child, "It really hurts me when you don't clean up you room." Or if you are a guilt-inducing partner in an intimate relationship, you might say to your partner, "It makes me angry when you go out every night of the week." Notice in both of these examples that the speaker is implying that the stimulus is the cause of the feelings: "You make me feel." "That makes me feel." "I'm feeling _____ because you _____."

In order to manage anger in ways that are in harmony with the principles of NVC, it's important to be conscious of this key distinction: *I feel as I do because I am telling myself thoughts about other people's actions that imply wrongness on their part.* Such thoughts take the form of judgments, such as, "I think they are selfish, I think the person is rude, or lazy, or manipulative, and they shouldn't do that." Such thoughts take either the form of direct judgment of others or indirect judgments expressed through such things as, "I'm judging them as thinking only they have something worth saying."

In these latter expressions, it's implicit that we think what the other person is doing isn't right. And that's important, because if I think this other person is making me feel this way, it's going to be hard for me not to imagine punishing them. NVC shows people that it's never what the other person does; instead, it's how you see it, how you interpret it. If people were to follow me around in my work, they would get some very significant learning in this area.

For example, I worked a lot in Rwanda. I often worked with people who had members of their family killed. Some were so angry that all they could do was wait for vengeance. They were furious. Other people in the same room had the same number of family members killed—maybe had even more killed—but they were not angry. They had strong feelings, but not anger. They had feelings that led them to want to prevent the killings from ever happening to others again, but not that led them to punish the other side. With NVC, we want people to see that it's how we look at the situation that *creates* our anger; it's not the stimulus itself.

With NVC training, I try to get people to see that when they're angry, it's because their consciousness is under the influence of the kind of language we all learned—that is, that the other side is evil or bad in some way.

This kind of thinking is the cause of anger. When this thinking happens, I show people not how to push it down and deny the anger or deny the thinking, but rather to transform it into a language of life, into a language in which they are much more likely to create peace between themselves and whoever acted in the way that stimulated their anger.

To do this, let's talk first about how to become conscious of the internalized thinking that's making you angry, how to transform it into what needs of yours have not been met by what the other person has done. Then let's look at how to proceed from that consciousness to creating peace again between you and that person.

The first step in expressing your anger—managing it in harmony with NVC—is to identify the stimulus for your anger without confusing it with your evaluation. The second step is to be conscious that it is your evaluation of people—in the form of judgments that imply wrongness—that causes your anger.

An Illustration of Stimulus Versus Cause of Anger

Once when I was working in a correctional school for delinquents, I had an experience that really helped me learn the lesson that it is never the stimulus that causes the anger. There is always, between the trigger and the anger, some thought process happening.

On two successive days, I had remarkably similar experiences, but each day I had quite different feelings in reaction to the experience. The experience in both situations involved my being hit in the nose, because on two successive days I was involved in breaking up a fight between two different pairs of students. And in both cases, as I was breaking up the fight, I caught an elbow in the nose.

On day one, I was furious. On day two, even though the nose was even sorer than it had been on the first day, I wasn't angry. Now, why would I be angry in response to the stimulus on day one, but not on day two?

First of all, in the first situation, if you had asked me right after I was hit in the nose why I was angry, I would have had trouble finding the thought that was making me angry. I probably would have said, "Well, I'm obviously angry because the child hit me in the nose." But that wasn't the cause. As I looked at the situation later, it was very clear to me that even before this incident, I had been thinking in very judgmental terms about the child whose elbow hit me in the nose. I had in my head a judgment of this child as a spoiled brat. So as soon as his elbow hit my nose, I was angry—it seemed that just as the elbow hit, I became angry. But between that stimulus and the anger, this image flashed within me of this child being a spoiled brat. Now, that all happened very fast, but it was the image of "spoiled brat" that made me angry.

On day two, I carried quite a different image of the child into the situation. Now I saw this child more as a pathetic creature than a spoiled brat; so when the elbow caught my nose, I wasn't angry. I certainly felt physical pain, but I wasn't angry, because a different image flashed through my mind: one of a child in great need of support rather than the judgmental image "spoiled brat" that had caused the anger.

These images happen very quickly, and they can easily trick us into thinking that the stimulus is the cause of our anger.

The Third Step

The third step in handling anger with NVC involves looking for the need that is the root of anger. This step is built on the assumption that we get angry because our needs are not getting met, and the problem is that we're not in touch with our needs. Instead of being directly connected to our need, we go up into our head and start thinking of what's wrong with other people for not meeting our needs. The judgments we make of other people—which cause our anger—are really *alienated expressions of unmet needs.*

Judgments

Over the years, I have come to see that these kinds of judgments of others that make us angry are not only alienated expressions of our needs; at times, they also look to me like suicidal, tragic expressions of our needs. Instead of going to our heart to connect to what we need and are not getting, we direct our attention to judging what is wrong with other people for not meeting our needs. When we do this, a couple of things are likely to happen.

First, our needs are not likely to get met, because when we verbally judge other people as being wrong in some way, these judgments usually create more defensiveness than learning or connection. At the very least, they don't create much cooperation. Even if people do things we would like them to do after we have judged them as being wrong or lazy or irresponsible, they will take these actions with an energy that we will pay for. We will pay for it because when we are angry as a result of judging people—and we express these judgments to them either verbally or through our nonverbal behavior—they pick up that we are judging them as being wrong in some way. Even if people then do what we would like them to do, they are likely to be motivated more out of fear of being punished, out of fear of being judged, or out of their guilt or shame than out of compassion in relation to our needs.

When we use NVC, however, we remain conscious at all times that why people do what we would like them to do is as important as the fact that they do it. So we are conscious that we only want people to do things willingly and not do things because they think they're going to be punished, blamed, guilted, or shamed if they don't.

Developing a Literacy of Needs

This practice requires developing a literacy and a consciousness of our needs. With a greater vocabulary of needs, we can more easily get in touch with the needs behind the judgments that are making us angry. It's when we can clearly express our needs that others have a much greater likelihood of responding compassionately to whatever it is we would like.

Let's go back to the case of the prisoner in Sweden. After we had identified the judgments he was making that were creating his anger, I asked him to look behind the judgments and tell me what needs of his were not getting met. These unmet needs were actually being expressed through the judgments he was making of the prison officials.

This wasn't easy for him to do, because when people are trained to think in terms of wrongness of others, they are often blind to what they themselves need. They often have very little vocabulary for describing their needs. It requires shifting attention away from judging outward to looking inward and seeing what the need is. But with some help, he was finally able to get in touch with his need, and he said, "Well, my need is to be able to take care of myself when I get out of prison by being able to get work. So the request that I was making of the prison officials was for training to meet that need. If I don't get that training, I'm not going to be able to take care of myself economically when I get out of prison, and I'm going to end up back in here."

Then I said to the prisoner, "Now that you're in touch with your need, how are you feeling?" He said, "I'm scared." So when we are directly connected to our need, we are *never* angry any more. The anger hasn't been repressed; the anger has been transformed into need-serving feelings.

The basic function of feelings is to serve our needs. The word *emotion* basically means to move us out, to mobilize us to meet our needs. When we have a need for some nourishment, we have a feeling that we label as hunger, and that sensation stimulates us to move about to take care of our need for food. If we just felt comfortable each time we had a need for nourishment, we could starve, because we wouldn't be mobilized to get our need met.

The natural function of emotions is to stimulate us to get our needs met. But anger is stimulated by a diversion. With anger, we are not in touch with the needs that would naturally motivate us to want to get our needs met. The anger is created by thinking about the wrongness of others, which transfers this energy away from seeking to get the need met and into an energy designed to blame and punish other people.

After I pointed out to the prisoner the difference between getting in touch with his needs and the feelings that he had, he became aware of his fear. He could see that the anger was because of him thinking about the wrongness of others. I then asked him, "Do you think you're more likely to get your needs met if, when you go to talk to the prison officials, you are connected to your needs and the fear, or if you are up in your head judging them and angry?"

He could see very clearly that he was much more likely to get his needs met if he were to communicate from a position of connection to his needs, rather than being separated from his needs and thinking of others in ways that implied wrongness. At the moment he had this insight into what a different world he would be living in if he stayed in touch with his needs as opposed to judging others, he looked down at the floor with one of the saddest looks I had ever seen.

I asked him, "What's going on?"

He said, "I can't talk about it right now." Later that day, he helped me understand. He came to me and said, "Marshall, I wish you could have taught me two years ago what you taught me this morning about anger. I wouldn't have had to kill my best friend."

Tragically, two years before, his best friend had done some things, and he felt great rage in response to his judgments about what his friend had done. But instead of being conscious of what his needs were behind all of that, he really thought it was his friend who had made him angry, and in a tragic interaction, he ended up killing the friend.

I'm not implying that every time we get angry we hurt or kill somebody. But I am suggesting that every time we are angry, we are disconnected from our needs. We are up in our head, thinking about the situation in a way that is going to make it very hard for us to get our needs met.

The step that I have just outlined is very important: we must be conscious of the thinking that is creating our anger. As I said, the prisoner at first was totally oblivious to all of the inner thoughts that were making him angry. The reason is that these thoughts go on very rapidly. Many of these thoughts go so quickly through our head, we are not even aware they are there. Instead, it seems as though it was the stimulus that caused our anger.

I have outlined three steps in managing anger using NVC:
1. Identify the stimulus for anger, without confusing it with the evaluation.
2. Identify the internal image or judgment that is making you angry.
3. Transform this judgmental image into the need that it is expressing; in other words, bring your full attention to the need that is behind the judgment.

These three steps are done internally—nothing is said out loud. Instead, you simply become aware that your anger is not caused by what the other person has done, but rather by your judgment. Then it's time to look for the need behind the judgment.

The Fourth Step

The fourth step in handling anger involves what is actually said out loud to the other person after anger has been transformed into other feelings by getting in touch with the need behind the judgment.

This fourth step includes saying to the other person four pieces of information. First, reveal the stimulus: what that person has done that is in conflict with your needs being fulfilled. Second, express how you are feeling. Notice you are not repressing the anger; instead, the anger has been transformed into a feeling, such as being sad, hurt, scared, frustrated, or the like. Then follow up the expression of your feelings with the needs of yours that are not being fulfilled.

And now we add to those three pieces of information *a clear, present request of what you want from the other person* in relationship to your feelings and unmet needs.

In the situation with the prisoner, his fourth step would be to go to the prison officials and say something like this: "I made a request three weeks ago. I still haven't heard from you. I'm feeling scared because I have a need to be able to earn a living when I leave this prison, and I'm afraid that without the training I was requesting, it will be very hard for me to make a living. So I'd like you to tell me what is preventing you from responding to my request."

Notice that for the prisoner to communicate in this way requires a lot of work on his part. He has to be conscious of what is going on inside him. He may require some help getting connected to his needs. In this situation, I was there to help him. But in NVC training, we show people how to do all of this for themselves.

When you're stimulated by another person and find yourself starting to get angry, it is important to manage that anger. If you're sufficiently trained in getting in touch with the need behind the judgments, you can take a deep breath and very rapidly go through the process that I led the prisoner through. So, as soon as you catch yourself getting angry, take a deep breath, stop, look inside, and ask yourself, "What am I telling myself that's making me so angry?" In this way, you can quickly get in touch with the need that is behind that judgment. When you're in touch with the need, you will feel in your body a shift away from anger to other kinds of feelings. Then, when you're at that point, you can say out loud to the other person what you're observing, feeling, and needing, and then you can make your requests.

This process takes practice, but with sufficient practice it can be done in a matter of seconds. Perhaps you're fortunate enough to have friends around who can help you get conscious about what's going on within you. If not, or until you are sufficiently trained, you can always take a time-out. Simply say to the person, "Time out. I need to do some work on myself right now, because I'm afraid that anything I say is going to get in the way of both of us getting our needs met." At this point, you can go off by yourself to get in touch with the needs behind your judgments that are making you angry. Then you can go back into the situation.

Once you can handle your own anger, it's very often advantageous to show some empathic understanding of what is going on in others that led them to behave as they did. By connecting to this *before* expressing yourself, the advantage can be even greater.

In managing your anger when it comes up this way, a key component is the ability to both identify the judgment making you angry and quickly transform it into the need that is behind the judgment. By practicing identifying judgments and translating them into needs, you can develop your ability to do this quickly in real situations. An exercise I recommend for practice is to list the kind of judgments that are likely to go on inside of you when you are angry. Perhaps think of the most recent time that you were angry and write down what you were telling yourself that was making you angry.

When you have made an inventory of the kinds of things you tell yourself in different situations that make you angry, go back over this list and ask yourself, "What was I needing that was being expressed through that judgment?" The more time you spend making these translations from judgments into needs, the more it will help you to quickly follow these procedures for expressing anger in real-life situations.

PUNISHMENT AND ANGER

I would like to add to this discussion of anger the concept of punishment. The kind of thinking that leads us to be angry is the kind of thinking that implies that people deserve to suffer for what they've done. In other words, I'm talking about the moralistic judgments we make of other people that imply wrongness, irresponsibility, or inappropriateness. At their root, all of these judgments imply that people shouldn't have done what they did and that they deserve some form of condemnation or punishment for doing it.

I believe you'll see that punishment can never really get needs met in a constructive way if you ask two questions. The first question is, *What do we want others to do differently from what they are now doing?* If we ask only this question, punishment may seem to work, because we may be able to get a child to stop hitting his sister if we punish him for doing it. Notice that I say it *may seem to* work, because often the very act of punishing people for what they do actually stimulates such antagonism that they continue to do it out of resentment or anger. They may even continue to do it longer than they would have done had there not been punishment.

But if I add a second question, I'm confident that you will see that punishment never works in the sense of getting needs met, at least not for reasons that we won't be sorry for later. The second question is, *What do we want the other person's reasons to be for doing what we want them to do?*

I think we can all agree that we never want other people to do things simply because they are afraid of punishment. We don't want them to do things out of obligation or duty, or out of guilt or shame, or to buy love. With some consciousness, I'm confident we all want people to do things only if they can do them willingly, because they clearly see how those things are going to enrich life if they do. Any other reason for doing things is likely to create conditions that make it harder for people in the future to behave in a compassionate way toward one another.

KILLING PEOPLE IS TOO SUPERFICIAL

Part of my objective is to show how the process of Nonviolent Communication can help you fully express your anger. This is very important to make clear with many of the groups that I work with. Usually when I'm invited into different countries, it's to work with groups that feel they have been very oppressed or discriminated against, and they want to increase the power that they have to change the situation. Very often such groups are a bit worried when they hear the term *Nonviolent Communication,* because very often in their history, they have been exposed to various religions and other trainings that have taught them to stifle their anger, to calm down and accept whatever is happening. As a consequence, they are rather worried about anything that tells them that their anger is bad or is something to be gotten rid of. It's a great relief for them when they come to really trust that the process I'm talking about in no way wants them to stifle anger, to repress it, to force it down. Instead, NVC is a way of fully expressing the anger.

I've often said that, to me, killing people is too superficial. To me, any kind of killing, blaming, punishing, or hurting other people is a very superficial expression of anger. We want something much more powerful than killing or hurting people physically or mentally. That's too weak. We want something much more powerful than that to fully express ourselves. The first step in being able to express our anger fully using Nonviolent Communication is to totally divorce the other person from any responsibility for our anger. As I've said, this means getting out of our consciousness any kind of thinking that he, she, they made us angry when they did that. When we think that way, we can be very dangerous, and we're not likely to fully express our anger. Instead, we're likely to superficially express anger by blaming or punishing the other person.

I have shown prisoners who want to punish others for what they do that vengeance is a distorted cry for empathy. When we think we need to hurt others, what we really need is for these other people to see how we have been hurt and to see how their behavior has contributed to our pain. Most of the prisoners I have worked with had never received that kind of empathy from people who had wronged them. So making those people suffer was the best they could think to do to find relief from their own pain.

I was demonstrating this once to a prisoner who told me he wanted to kill this man. I said, "I bet I can show you something that would be sweeter than vengeance."

The prisoner said, "No way, man. The only thing that's kept me alive these last two years in prison is thinking of getting out and getting this guy for what he did to me. That's the only thing in the world I want. They're gonna put me back in here, and that's OK. All I want to do is get out and really hurt this guy."

I said, "I bet I can show you something more delicious than that."

"No way, man."

"Would you give me some time?"

(I liked this guy's sense of humor. He said, "I got plenty of time, man," and he was going to be there for a while. That's why I like working with prisoners: they're not running off to appointments.)

Anyway, I said, "What I'd like to show you is another option besides hurting people. I'd like you to play the role of the other person."

MARSHALL: It's the first day I'm out of prison. I find you. The first thing I do is I grab you.

PRISONER, AS HIMSELF: That's a good start

MARSHALL: I put you in a chair, and I say, "I'm gonna tell you some things, and I want you to tell me back what you heard me say. You got that?"

PRISONER, IN OTHER PERSON'S ROLE: But I can explain it!

MARSHALL, AS PRISONER: Shut up. Did you hear what I said? I want you to tell me back what you hear me say.

PRISONER, AS OTHER PERSON: OK.

MARSHALL, AS PRISONER: I took you into my house and treated you as a brother. I gave you everything for eight months, and then you did what you did to me. I was so hurt I could hardly stand it.

[I had heard the prisoner talk about this several times, so it was not hard for me to play his role.]

PRISONER, AS OTHER PERSON: But I can explain it!

MARSHALL, AS PRISONER: Shut up. Tell me what you heard.

PRISONER, AS OTHER PERSON: After all you had done for me, you felt really hurt. You would have liked something else besides what happened.

MARSHALL, AS PRISONER: And then, do you know what it's like for the next two years to be angry day and night so that nothing would satisfy me, except thoughts of hurting you?

PRISONER, AS OTHER PERSON: So it really got your whole life screwed up so that all you could do was be consumed with anger for two years?

We kept this going for another few minutes, and then this man became very emotionally moved. He said, "Stop, stop, you're right. That's what I need."

The next time I went to that prison, about a month later, a changed guy was waiting for me as I came through the gate. He was pacing back and forth, and he said, "Hey Marshall, remember the last time you said that when we really think that we enjoy hurting people or we want to hurt somebody, the real need is for understanding for how we've suffered?"

I said, "Yeah, I remember that."

"Would you go over that again today real slow? I'm getting out of here in three days, and if I don't get this clear somebody's gonna get hurt."

So my prediction is that anybody who enjoys hurting others is being exposed to a lot of violence themselves—psychological or otherwise. And they need empathy for the enormous pain that they're feeling.

WORKSHOP INTERACTIONS

Again, the first step to get into our consciousness is realizing that *what other people do is never the cause of how we feel*. What is the cause of how we feel? It's my belief that how we feel is a result of how we interpret the behavior of others at any given moment. If I ask you to pick me up at six o'clock, and you pick me up at six thirty, how do I feel? It depends on how I look at it. That you were thirty minutes later than you said you would be doesn't make me feel whatever I feel; it's how I choose to interpret it. If I choose to put on my judging ears, then they're perfect for playing the game of who's right, who's wrong, who's at fault. If I put these ears on, I will find somebody at fault. So it's how we interpret the behavior and what meaning we ascribe to it that causes our feelings.

There's another connection to feelings, and that's the other choice. If I put on my NVC ears, my thinking does not go to who's at fault. I do not go up into my head and make a mental analysis of the wrongness on either my part or your part.

These NVC ears can help us connect to life, to the life that is going on within ourselves. And to me, this life that is going on within can be most clearly revealed or grasped by looking at what our needs are. So, ask yourself, "What are my needs in this situation?" When you are connected to your needs, you may have strong feelings, but never anger.

Anger is a result of life-alienated thinking, or thinking that is disconnected from needs. Anger says that you have gone up into your head and have chosen to analyze the wrongness of the other person, and that you are disconnected from your needs. But your needs are really the stimulus of what's going on—they are the stimulus of the anger you are feeling. You are not conscious of what you need; your consciousness is focused on what's wrong with the other person for not meeting your needs. But if you connect to the other person's needs, you will never feel angry. This doesn't mean that you are *repressing* your anger; you simply won't feel it.

I'm suggesting that how we feel each moment is a result of which of these four options we choose: Do we choose to go up into our head and judge the other person? Do we choose to go up into our head and judge ourselves? Do we choose to connect empathically with the other person's needs? Or do we choose to connect empathically with our needs? It is that choice that determines our feelings. That's why Nonviolent Communication requires that a very important word come after the word *because*—the word *I*, not the word *you*. For instance, "I feel angry because I _____." This reminds us that what we feel is not because of what the other person did, but because of the choice we made.

Remember that I see all anger as a result of life-alienated, violence-provocative thinking. I think all anger is righteous in the sense that to fully express the anger means putting our entire consciousness on the need that isn't getting met. There is a need that isn't getting met, and that's righteous; I mean we have a *right* to the feeling in the sense that a need is not getting met. We have to get that need met, and we require the energy to motivate us to get the need met. However, I'm also suggesting that anger distorts that energy away from the direction of fulfilling the needs into punitive action, and, in that sense, it's a destructive energy.

FROM PHILOSOPHICAL TO TACTICAL TO PRACTICAL

Let me show you that what I'm talking about is more tactical than philosophical. To explain what I mean by tactical, let's go back to that prisoner example. I wasn't trying to sell the NVC process to him on philosophical principles, but on tactical principles.

When he said that the prison officials hadn't responded to his request, I asked, "OK, so what made you angry?" And he said, "I told you. They didn't respond to my request." I said, "Stop. Don't say, 'I felt angry because *they* . . .' Stop and become conscious of what you were telling yourself that was making *you* so angry." But he wasn't of the philosophical or psychological background; he wasn't used to sorting out what was going on inside.

So I said, "Stop. Slow down. Just listen. What's going on inside?"

And then it came out: "I'm telling myself that they have no respect for human beings. They're a bunch of cold, faceless bureaucrats."

He was going to continue, but I said. "Stop. That's enough, that's enough. That's why you're angry."

Then I said to him, "It's that kind of thinking on your part that is making you feel very angry. So focus your attention on your needs. What are you needs in this situation?"

He thought for a while, and he said, "Marshall, I need the training I was requesting. If I don't get that training, as sure as I'm sitting here, I'm going to end up back in this prison when I get out."

PARTICIPANT U: What you're saying makes sense to me, but I feel like it requires being so superhuman on my part. It seems like the anger is so instantaneous, and to actually be able to think through these different steps seems to require me to be much bigger than I am.

MARSHALL: All it requires is to shut up. I don't see that as being so superheroic. All it requires is to shut up. Don't say anything intended to blame the other person at that moment and don't take any actions to punish the other person. Just stop and do nothing except breathe and take these steps. First—and it's a big step—just shut up.

PARTICIPANT U: But in your earlier example, when you were waiting a half-hour for a person to pick you up—I mean, they don't even have to be there, and I'm already stewing, thinking, you know, "I can't believe he didn't pick me up. Doesn't he ever remember anything I ask," and on and on and on.

MARSHALL: What I'm saying is there's something you could be doing during that time to relieve yourself and that will also increase the likelihood that you'll get your needs met. If you do these steps that we're talking about, you will have something you can say when he gets there (or she gets there) that is more likely to get him to be on time the next time. I hope I can make it clear so it doesn't seem superhuman. Superhuman is to try to suppress the anger, to try to push it down. What we're really aiming for is to keep our attention connected to life moment by moment. We connect to the life that's going on in us, what our needs are at this moment, and focus our attention on the life that's going on in other people.

Example of One Woman's Anger

PARTICIPANT V: I faced a situation in which I was in a conversation with someone and a third person joined the conversation and started addressing the other person without me. He then made a comment to the effect that they preferred people in their community to be white. I felt so angry, because I wasn't getting my need met to continue to enjoy the conversation I was having.

MARSHALL: Now, hold on. I doubt that—I doubt that that's why you got angry. See, I don't think we get angry because our needs aren't getting met. I'll bet you got angry because you had some thoughts about that other person at that moment. So I'd like you to be conscious right now about what you were telling yourself that made you so angry about that person.

So here's a person who says, "I'd rather have only white people here," and he addresses somebody else rather than you. And you felt angry because why? Because you told yourself what?

PARTICIPANT V: Well, I asked myself, "What's this person doing, taking over the conversation that I was already having?"

MARSHALL: Think behind the question, "What is this person doing?" What do you think of a person for doing that?

PARTICIPANT V: Well, it's not a good thought.

MARSHALL: But I think it's in there. I'm not trying to make you have certain thoughts. I'm just wanting to make you conscious of what I predict is in there. It probably all happened so fast.

PARTICIPANT V: No, right away I was feeling left out.

MARSHALL: Well, that's coming closer. So you interpreted him as leaving you out. Notice how the image "left out" is not a feeling. It's an interpretation. It's like being abandoned: "I'm feeling abandoned." "I'm feeling unnoticed." So it's really more an image; you had this image of being left out. And what else was going on there?

PARTICIPANT V: I think it was more than an image, because he was making eye contact and talking to the other person, and in that exchange they were not talking to me.

MARSHALL: But I think there are twenty different ways we could look at that, of which leaving you out is only one. There are many other possible ways of interpreting that. And each one is going to have a big impact on how you feel. So let's slow down again. What other thoughts were going on in you that made you angry at that moment?

PARTICIPANT V: Well, I had thoughts associated with somebody using the word *white*.

MARSHALL: Yeah, I think we're getting closer now. So, what is your image when somebody uses the word *white* in that way? Especially when he doesn't look at you but he looks at others?

PARTICIPANT V: What I told myself was when they say *white*, they don't mean me.

MARSHALL: So they're kind of excluding you.

PARTICIPANT V: And, in fact, their behavior and body language and everything was also giving me that message.

MARSHALL: So you believe they were excluding you because of race? Do you have any thoughts about people who do that?

PARTICIPANT V: Yeah, a lot, I mean . . .

MARSHALL: That's what I'm trying to get at. I'm thinking it's those thoughts that got stimulated in that moment by that action and that's what made you angry.

PARTICIPANT V: I think so. I agree with what you're saying. I think it was both that and the fact that I was actually being excluded.

MARSHALL: No, you weren't actually being excluded. That was your interpretation that you were being excluded. The fact—and I'm defining this observation as a fact—is that the person had eye contact with others. See, that's the fact. Whether you interpret that as excluding you, whether you interpret that as racist, whether you interpret that as that person being frightened of you—these are all interpretations. The fact is, he didn't look at you. The fact is, he said something about *white*. Those are the facts. But if you interpret it as excluding, already you are going to be provoking different feelings in yourself than if you look at it in other ways.

PARTICIPANT U: So how could she have handled that? The body language was excluding her; the conversation was excluding her. I mean, how does she get to her needs?

MARSHALL: If her objective is to fully express her anger, I would suggest that she become conscious of this thing that we're struggling with now, that she become conscious of what she's telling herself that is making her so angry. So, in this case, it sounds like she got angry because she immediately interpreted herself being excluded on the basis of race. This raised all kinds of thoughts in her about "That isn't right. You shouldn't exclude people on the basis of race." Was that kind of deeply in there?

PARTICIPANT V: I think that came a little later. Yeah, my immediate experience was that I felt invisible and bewildered and confused. I didn't understand why that was happening.

MARSHALL: Yeah, so your immediate response in this case wasn't to judge the other person. The immediate one was that you were confused, bewildered. You had a need for some understanding: "Why is this happening?" Then the thinking started to go off.

PARTICIPANT V: That's when the anger started.

MARSHALL: Then the anger started to come because you started to have some hypotheses about why it was happening. And you wanted to fully express this anger that came from interpreting: "Hey, wait a minute, I think they are excluding me on the basis of race, and I don't like that. I think that's racist. I don't think that's fair. I don't think a person should be excluded on that basis." Thoughts like that.

PARTICIPANT V: Yeah.

MARSHALL: OK, now that's the second step. First step, be quiet and identify the thoughts that are making us angry. Next, get connected to the needs behind those thoughts. So when you say to yourself, "I don't think a person should be excluded on a basis of race. I think that's unfair. I think that's racist," I'm suggesting all judgments—and *racist* would be a good example—are tragic expressions of unmet needs.

So what is the need behind the judgment *racist?* If I judge somebody as a racist, what is my need? I would like to be included; I would like there to be equality. I would like to be given the same respect and consideration as anybody else.

To fully express my anger, I open my mouth and say all that, because now the anger has been transformed into my needs and need-connected feelings. And yet the need-connected feelings are much scarier for me to express than the anger.

"That was a racist thing to do." That is not hard for me to say at all. I kind of like saying that. But it's really scary for me to get down to what's behind that feeling, because feelings for me are so deeply related to racism that it's scary—but that's fully expressing the anger.

So then I might open my mouth and say to the person, "When you came into the group just now and started to talk to others and not say anything to me, and then when I heard the comment about *white,* I felt really sick to my stomach and really scared. It just triggered off all kinds of needs on my part to be treated equally, and I'd like you to tell me how you feel when I tell you this."

PARTICIPANT V: Actually, I did have something like that conversation with the person. And some of my frustration and anger that hasn't gone away is that I could get only so far with it. I get the feeling that there's this whole range of experiences that I've had that he wasn't comprehending.

MARSHALL: So if I'm hearing you right, you're afraid that the other person did not really connect with and understand all that was going on for you in that experience?

PARTICIPANT V: Right. And then there's a buildup over years of what I guess I would call rage about that gap in understanding.

Getting Understanding from Others About Our Feelings and Needs

MARSHALL: We want to get some understanding from that person. So fully expressing the anger means not just that I express these deep feelings behind it, but that I also help this person to get it.

To do this, we have to develop some skills, because if we want understanding from such a person, the best way to get it is to give this person the understanding first. See, the more I empathize with what led this person to behave this way, the greater the likelihood that I'll be able afterward to get him to reciprocate and hear all of this depth of experience that I have. It's going to be pretty hard for him to hear it. So if I want him to hear it, I need to first empathize.

Let me give you an idea of how that goes in a situation like this. For the past thirty years, I've had a lot of experience with racism, because I started off using NVC with people with strong racial positions. Unfortunately, to this day, in many of the countries where I work, this is the number one thing that citizens are concerned with. In many countries in the world, skinheads and other groups of neofascists are making it very unsafe to move about. This is a very big issue, so we need to get very good at getting these people to understand.

Anyway, early one morning, a cab picked up me and another person at the airport to take us into town. Over the cabbie's loudspeaker, we heard, "Pick up Mr. Fishman at the synagogue on such and such street." The man sitting next to me said, "These kikes get up early in the morning so they can screw everybody out of their money." I had smoke coming out of my ears, because it takes far less than that to make a maniac out of me. For many years, my first reaction would have been to physically hurt this person. So for about twenty seconds, I had to take deep breaths and give myself some empathy for all the hurt, fear, rage, and more that was going on in me.

So I listened to that. I was conscious that my anger wasn't coming from him; it was not coming from his statement. My anger—the depth of my fear—could not be stimulated by such a statement. It went far deeper than that. I knew it had nothing to do with his statement; it just triggered me to want to blow up like a volcano.

So I sat back and just enjoyed this judgment show going on in my head. I enjoyed the images of taking his head and smashing it.

And then the first words out of my mouth were, "Are you feeling and needing?" I wanted to empathize with him. I wanted to hear his pain. Why? Because I wanted him to get it. I wanted him to see what was going on in me when he said that. But I've learned that if I want that kind of understanding of what goes on in me, other people will not be able to hear it if they have a storm going on in them. So I wanted to connect and show a respectful empathy for the life energy in him that was behind that comment, because my experience told me that if I did that he would be able to hear me. It wouldn't be easy, but he would be able to hear me.

I said, "It sounds like you had some bad experiences with Jewish people."

And he looked at me. "Yeah," he said. "Those people are disgusting. They'll do anything for money."

"Sounds like you have a lot of distrust, and you need to protect yourself when you're with them about financial affairs."

"Yes."

So he kept going on with it. And I kept hearing his feelings and needs.

Now, you know, when you put your attention on other people's feelings and needs, there's no conflict. Because what were his feelings and needs? When I heard that he was scared and wanted to protect himself, I could understand. I have those needs. I have a need to protect myself. I know what it's like to be scared. When my con-sciousness is on another human being's feelings and needs, I see the universality of all of our experiences. I may have a big conflict with what goes on in someone's head, with his way of thinking, but I've learned that I enjoy human beings much better when I don't hear what they think. I've learned—especially with folks who have these kinds of thoughts—that I can enjoy life much more if I hear what's going on in their heart and not get caught up with the stuff that comes out of the head.

So, after awhile this guy was just really pouring out his sadness and frustration. Before we knew it, he got off the topic of Jews and moved on to blacks and some other groups. The guy had a lot of pain about all kinds of stuff.

After maybe ten minutes of my just listening, he stopped. He felt understood. And then I let him know what was going on in me.

I said, "You know, when you first started to talk, I felt a lot of frustra-tion and discouragement, because I've had quite a different experience with Jews than you've had, and I was really wanting you to have much more the experience that I have had. Can you tell me what you heard me say?"

"Well, look, I'm not saying they're all . . ."

I said, "Excuse me. Hold it, hold it. Could you tell me what you heard me say?"

"What are you talking about?"

"Let me say again what I'm trying to say. I want you to hear, really hear, the pain that I felt when I heard your words. It's really important for me that you hear that. I said I felt a real sense of sadness, because I've had such different experiences with Jewish people, and I was just wishing that you could share a different experience than you've had. Can you tell me what you've heard me say?"

"Well, you're saying I have no right to say that."

I replied, "No, I really don't want to blame you. Really, I don't have any desire to blame you."

See, if he was hearing any amount of blame, then he did not get it. If he had said, "It was a terrible thing for me to say, that was a racist thing for me to say, I shouldn't have said it," that still means he didn't get it. If he heard that he did anything wrong, he didn't get it. I wanted him to hear the pain that happened in my heart when he said those things. I wanted him to see what needs of mine were not met when he said that. I did not want to blame him. That's too easy.

So we have to work for that—we have to pull the judging person by the ears. Here's why: people who judge are not too used to hearing feelings and needs. They're used to hearing blame, and then they either agree with it and hate themselves, which doesn't stop them from continuing to behave that way, or they hate you for calling them a racist, which doesn't stop them from behaving that way. So that's what I mean by needing the other person to get it. You may have to hear their pain for a while first.

Of course, before I could hear such people's pain, I had to do a lot of work for years. A lot of work!

PARTICIPANT V: I still feel like I want to be able to protect myself. In other words, if I had a choice, I just wouldn't interact with the person, but since he got in my space, I kind of got involved. And so I'm not sure what you're trying to say.

MARSHALL: What I'm saying is that if we want to fully express our anger to the person, then I would go through this. But I'm not saying I *always* want to fully express my anger to such a person. Very often my need might be to go talk to somebody else about this, to ignore this person. But if I really wanted to fully express my anger to him, I would give him the empathy that he would need to be able to hear the depth of feelings and needs that go on in me when that behavior occurs. That's the best way I have found to really fully express my anger, to really let this person know the depth of what's going on in me. As you point out, it's not enough to just pour that out. I need him to get it; I need him to hear it empathically. That doesn't mean he has to agree; he doesn't even have to change his behavior. I just need him to hear what goes on in me. So for twenty seconds in the cab, I had a whole lifetime of stuff floating in, and I sat back and enjoyed it.

Enjoying the Judgment Show in Your Head

Here's what goes on in me in these situations. Not long ago I was in one country, and somebody was coming at me pretty hard in a judging kind of way. This person was going blah, blah, blah, and saying some very judgmental things toward me, and here was my reaction.

[Marshall is silent for a while.]

Then I said, "So, you're feeling really annoyed, and you would have liked so and so."

The person says, "Yes and blah, blah, blah."

And here's my reaction.

[Marshall is silent again.]

And then I said, "So it sounds like you were feeling some hurt behind that because you would have liked blah, blah, blah."

"Yes, and blah, blah, blah."

Anyway, this went on several times, and after this stopped a woman said to me, "Marshall, I've never seen a person more compassionate than you are. If somebody had talked to me the way you were being talked to there, I would've hit them. How did you do it?"

I said, "Let me tell you what was going on in me. You remember that first statement?"

"Yes."

"Here's my first reaction: 'If you don't shut up, I'm going to jam your head up your #@$#. In fact, you've got your head so far up there, you need a cellophane navel to see.'"

And then I said to the woman, "And it got worse from there. I mean, then I had some really graphic images, and I started to realize that this person's statements were very like some ridicule that I had experienced as a child. I realized that behind that reaction, I had a lot of fear and all of that. I went from this rage and wanting to shake her to being aware of the humiliation behind it. So I just stopped and listened. And when I got to that humiliation, that fear of being humiliated, I felt a release in my body. Then I could do what you heard me say, when I shifted my attention and put it on her feelings and needs.

"And then you remember the second statement she hit me with?"

And this other person said, "Yes."

I said, "Here was my first reaction."

And when I told her my first reaction, this woman's eyes get very big. She says, "I never knew you were so violent." So I have gone from being very compassionate to very violent in just a couple of exchanges.

Well, they're both there. There's an enormous amount of violence in me, conditioned by cultural factors and other things. So I enjoy that. I just sit back when I get that angry, and I watch this violent show going on in my head. I hear all these violent things I'd like to say, and I see these things I'd like to do to this person, and then I listen to the pain that's behind it. And when I get to the pain behind it, there's always a release.

Then I can put my attention on the other person's humanness.

I'm not repressing anything—quite the opposite. I'm enjoying it, this show going on, this violent show going in my head. I'm just not acting on it, because to act on it is too superficial. If I jump in and blame others, we're never going to get down to the pain behind all this. I'm not going to really be able to fully express my needs to them and have them get it. We'll just get into a fight, and I know how that ends: even when I win, I don't feel good. So, no, I want to fully express what's going on in me.

Take Your Time

PARTICIPANT W: You've mentioned before that this is a slow process. You mention that you need time; you take time to give yourself empathy. Well, if you're trying to have a conversation and also deal with that time, it seems to me that you have to tell the other person, "Wait a minute. I'm thinking before I can answer." I mean, because you may think more slowly so you can respond.

MARSHALL: Yes. As I mentioned earlier, I carry with me a picture of a my friend's son, who was wearing a T-shirt that says *Take Your Time*. That picture of that boy in his shirt is a very powerful symbol to me. It's probably the most important part for me in learning this process, learning how to live by it. Take your time.

Yes, it feels awkward at times not to behave out of the automatic way I was trained, but I want to take my time so that I live my life in harmony with my own values instead of in a robotlike way, automatically carrying out the way I was programmed by the culture in which I was raised. So, yes, take your time. It may feel awkward, but for me it's my life. I'm going to take my time to live it in a way I want—even if I look silly.

A friend of mine, Sam Williams, put this process on a three-by-five card—the kind that the Center for Nonviolent Conversation now sells (we got the idea from Sam). He would use this as a cheat sheet at work. The boss would come at him in a judging way, and he would take his time. He would stop and look down at this card in his hand and remember how to respond.

And I said, "Sam, don't people think you're a little weird looking down at your hand and taking all of that time?"

He said, "Actually, it doesn't take me that much time. But, even so, I don't care. I want to really make sure that I'm responding as I want to respond."

But at home, he was overt about it. He explained to his children and to his wife why he had this card, and he said, "I may look strange, and I may take a lot of time. But this is why I'm doing it." So when they would have these arguments at home, he would take his time. And after about a month, he felt comfortable enough to put the card away.

Then one night he and his four-year-old son, Scotty, were having a conflict about the television, and it wasn't going well. And Scotty said, "Daddy, get the card."

ANGER SOUND BITES

How I choose to look at that situation will greatly affect whether I have the power to change it or make matters worse.

There's not a thing another person can do that can make me angry.

Any thinking that is in my head that involves the word *should* is violence-provoking.

I don't think we get angry because our needs aren't getting met. I think we get angry because we have judgments about others.

Anger is a natural feeling created by unnatural thinking.

I'm not saying that it is wrong to judge people. What's important is to be conscious that it's that judgment that makes us angry.

Even if you don't say judgments out loud, your eyes show this kind of thinking.

Use the words "I feel because I . . ." to remind yourself that what you feel is not because of what the other person did, but because of the choice you made.

To me, the life that's going on within us can be most clearly grasped by looking at what our needs are. Ask yourself, "What are my needs in this situation?"

When I am connected to my needs, I have strong feelings but never anger. I see all anger as a result of life-alienated, violent, provocative thinking.

Killing people is too superficial. To me, any kind of killing, blaming, or hurting of other people is a very superficial expression of our anger.

Our aim is to keep our attention, moment by moment, connected to life, to the life that's going on in us. What are our needs at this moment, and what's alive in others?

Sadness is a feeling that mobilizes us to get our needs met. Anger is a feeling that mobilizes us to blame and punish others.

Fully expressing the anger means not only that I express these deep feelings behind it but also that I help the other person to get it.

THE SURPRISING PURPOSE OF ANGER

To fully express anger means getting our full consciousness tuned in to the need that isn't getting met.

The best way I can get understanding from others is to give them understanding, too. If I want them to hear my needs and feelings, I first need to empathize.

When I give people the empathy they need, I've found it isn't that hard to get them to hear me.

Anger is a very valuable feeling in NVC. It's a wake-up call. It tells me that I'm thinking in ways almost guaranteed not to meet my needs. Why? Because my energy is not connected to my needs, and I'm not even aware of what my needs are when I'm angry. [*]

5

RAISING CHILDREN COMPASSIONATELY

Parenting the
Nonviolent Communication Way

We've been teaching Nonviolent Communication to parents for more than thirty years. I would like to share some of the things that have been helpful to me and to the parents I've worked with, as well as to share with you some insights I've had into the wonderful and challenging occupation of parenting.

I'd first like to call your attention to the danger of the word *child* when we allow it to apply a different quality of respect than we would give to someone who is not labeled a child. Let me show you what I am referring to.

In parent workshops that I've done over the years, I've often started by dividing the group into two. I put one group in one room and the other in a different room, and I give each group the task of writing down on a large piece of paper a dialogue between themselves and another person in a conflict situation. I tell both groups what the conflict is. The only difference is that I tell one group that the other person is their child, and to the second group I say that the other person is their neighbor.

Then we get back into a large group, and we look at these different sheets of paper outlining the dialogue that the groups would have. (I do not allow the groups to know who the person in the other group's situation was, so that both groups think the situation is the same.)

After they've had a chance to scan the written dialogues of both groups, I ask them if they can see a difference in terms of the degree of respect and compassion. Every time I've done this, the group that was working on the situation with the other person being a child was seen as being less respectful and compassionate in their communication than the group that saw the other person as a neighbor. This painfully reveals to the people in these groups how easy it is to dehumanize someone by the simple process of thinking of him or her as "our child."

MY OWN AWARENESS

I had an experience one day that really heightened my awareness of the danger of thinking of people as children. This experience followed a weekend in which I had worked with two groups: a street gang and a police department. I was mediating between the two groups. There had been considerable violence between them, and they had asked that I serve in the role of mediator. After spending as much time as I did with them, dealing with the violence they had toward one another, I was exhausted. As I was driving home afterward, I told myself, "I never want to be in the middle of another conflict for the rest of my life."

Of course, when I walked in my back door, my three children were fighting. I expressed my pain to them in a way that we advocate in Nonviolent Communication. I expressed how I was feeling, what my needs were, and what my requests were. I did it this way. I shouted, "When I hear all of this going on right now, I feel extremely tense! I have a real need for some peace and quiet after the weekend I've been through! So would you all be willing to give me that time and space?"

My oldest son looked at me and said, "Would you like to talk about it?" Now, at that moment, I dehumanized him in my thinking. Why? Because I said to myself, "How cute. Here's a nine-year-old boy trying to help his father." But take a closer look at how I was disregarding his offer because of his age, because I had him labeled as a child. Fortunately I saw that this was going on in my head, and maybe I was able to see it more clearly because the work I had been doing between the street gang and the police showed me the danger of thinking of people in terms of labels instead of their humanness.

So instead of seeing him as a child and thinking to myself, "How cute," I saw a human being who was reaching out to another human being in pain, and I said out loud, "Yes, I would like to talk about it." And the three of them followed me into another room and listened while I opened up my heart to how painful it was to see that people could come to a point of wanting to hurt one another simply because they hadn't been trained to see the other person's humanness. After talking about it for forty-five minutes, I felt wonderful, and, as I recall, we turned the stereo on and danced like fools for a while.

OUR EDUCATION AS PARENTS

I'm not suggesting that we don't use words like *child* as a shorthand way of letting people know that we're talking about people of a certain age. I'm talking about when we allow labels like this to keep us from seeing the other person as a human being, in a way that leads us to dehumanize the other person because of the things our culture teaches us about "children." Let me show you an extension of what I'm talking about, how the label *child* can lead us to behave in a way that's quite unfortunate.

Having been educated as I was to think about parenting, I thought that it was the job of a parent to make children behave. You see, once you define yourself as an authority—a teacher or parent—in the culture that I was educated in, you then see it as your responsibility to make people that you label a "child" or a "student" behave in a certain way.

I now see what a self-defeating objective this is, because I have learned that any time it's our objective to get another person to behave in a certain way, people are likely to resist, no matter what it is we're asking. This seems to be true whether the other person is two or ninety-two years of age.

This objective of getting what we want from other people—or getting them to do what we want them to do—threatens the autonomy of people, their right to choose what they want to do. And whenever people feel that they're not free to choose what they want to do, they are likely to resist, even if they see the purpose in what we are asking and would ordinarily want to do it. So strong is our need to protect our autonomy that if we see that someone has this single-mindedness of purpose, if they are acting like they think they know what's best for us but are not leaving it to us to make the choice of how we behave, it stimulates our resistance.

THE LIMITATIONS OF COERCION AND PUNISHMENT

I'll be forever grateful to my children for educating me about the limitations of the objective of getting other people to do what you want.

They taught me that, first of all, I couldn't make them do what I wanted. I couldn't make them do anything. I couldn't make them put a toy back in the toy box. I couldn't make them make their beds. I couldn't make them eat. That was quite a humbling lesson for me as a parent—to learn about my powerlessness—because somewhere I had gotten it into my mind that it was the job of a parent to make a child behave. And here were these young children teaching me this humbling lesson: that I couldn't make them do anything. All I could do was make them wish they had. Whenever I would be foolish enough to do that—that is, to make them wish they had—they taught me a second lesson about parenting and power that has proven very valuable to me over the years. And that lesson was that any time I would make them wish they had, they would make me wish I hadn't made them wish they had. Violence begets violence.

They taught me that any use of coercion on my part would invariably create resistance on their part, which could lead to an adversarial quality in the connection between us. I don't want to have that quality of connection with any human being, but especially not with my children, those human beings I'm closest to and taking responsibility for. So my children are the last people with whom I want to get into these coercive games of which punishment is a part.

This concept of punishment is strongly advocated by most parents. Studies indicate that about eighty percent of American parents firmly believe in corporal punishment of children. This is about the same percentage of the population that believes in capital punishment of criminals. With such a high percentage of the population believing that punishment is justified and necessary in the education of children, I've had plenty of opportunity over the years to discuss this issue with parents, and I'm pleased by how people can be helped to see the limitations of any kind of punishment if they'll simply ask themselves two questions.

Question number one: *What do we want the child to do differently?* If we ask only that question, it can certainly seem that punishment sometimes works, because certainly through the threat of punishment or application of punishment, we can at times influence a child to do what we would like the child to do.

However, when we add a second question, it has been my experience that parents see that punishment never works. The second question is, *What do we want the child's reasons to be for acting as we would like them to act?* It's this question that helps us to see that punishment not only doesn't work, but it also gets in the way of our children doing things for reasons that we would like them to do things.

Since punishment is so frequently used and justified, parents can only imagine that the opposite of punishment is a kind of permissiveness in which we do nothing when children behave in ways that are not in harmony with our values. Therefore, parents can think only, "If I don't punish, then I give up my own values and just allow the child to do whatever she wants." As I'll be discussing below, there are other approaches besides permissiveness or coercive tactics such as punishment.

While I'm at it, I'd like to suggest that reward is just as coercive as punishment. In both cases, we are using power *over* people, controlling the environment in a way that tries to force people to behave in ways that we like. In that respect, reward comes out of the same mode of thinking as punishment.

A CERTAIN QUALITY OF CONNECTION

There is another approach besides doing nothing or using coercive tactics. It requires an awareness of the subtle but important difference between our objective being to get people to do what we want, which I'm not advocating, and instead being clear that our objective is to create the quality of connection necessary for everyone's needs to be met.

It has been my experience, whether communicating with children or adults, that when we see the difference between these two objectives—when we are consciously not trying to get a person to do what we want but trying to create a quality of mutual concern, of mutual respect, a quality where both parties think that their needs matter and they are conscious that their needs and the other person's well-being are interdependent—it is amazing how conflicts that otherwise seem irresolvable are easily resolved.

The kind of communication that is involved in creating the quality of connection necessary for everybody's needs to get met is quite different from the communication used in coercive forms of resolving differences with children. It requires a shift away from evaluating children in moralistic terms, such as right/wrong or good/bad, to a language based on needs. We have to be able to tell children whether what they're doing is in harmony with our needs or in conflict with our needs, but we have to do it in a way that doesn't stimulate guilt or shame on the child's part. So it might require saying to the child, "I'm scared when I see you hitting your brother, because I have a need for people in the family to be safe," instead of, "It's wrong to hit your brother." Or it might require a shift away from saying, "You are lazy for not cleaning up your room," to saying, "I feel frustrated when I see that the bed isn't made, because I have a real need for support in keeping order in the house."

This shift in language away from classifying children's behavior in terms of right or wrong and good or bad to a language based on needs is not easy for those of us who were educated by teachers and parents to think in moralistic judgments. It also requires an ability to be present to our children and to listen to them with empathy when they are in distress. This is not easy when we have been trained as parents to want to jump in and give advice or to try to fix things.

When I'm working with parents, we look at situations that are likely to arise in which a child might say something like, "Nobody likes me." When children say something like that, I believe they need an empathic kind of connection. By that, I mean a respectful understanding in which they feel that we are there and really hear what they are feeling and needing. Sometimes we can do this silently, just by showing in our eyes that we are with their feelings of sadness and their need for a different quality of connection with their friends. Or it could involve our saying out loud something like, "So it sounds like you're really feeling sad, because you aren't having very much fun with your friends."

But many parents, defining their role as requiring them to make their children happy all the time, jump in when a child says something like that, and they say things like, "Well, have you looked at what you've been doing that might have been driving your friends away?" Or they disagree with the child, saying, "Well, that's not true. You've had friends in the past. I'm sure you'll get more friends." Or they give advice: "Maybe if you'd talk differently to your friends, your friends would like you more."

What they don't realize is that all human beings, when they're in pain, need presence and empathy. We may want advice, but we want that after we've received the empathic connection. My own children have taught this to me the hard way by telling me, "Dad, please withhold all advice unless you receive a request in writing from us signed by a notary."

THE LIMITATIONS OF REWARDS

Many people believe that it's more humane to use reward than punishment. But I see both of them as power *over* others, and Nonviolent

Communication is based on power *with* people. In power *with* people, we try to have influence not by how we can make people suffer if they don't do what we want or how we can reward them if they do. Instead, it's a power based on mutual trust and respect, which makes people open to hearing one another, learning from one another, and giving to one another willingly out of a desire to contribute to one another's well-being, rather than out of a fear of punishment or hope for a reward.

We get this kind of power—power *with* people—by being able to openly communicate our feelings and needs without in any way criticizing others. We do that by offering what we would like from them in a way that is not heard as demanding or threatening. And as I have said, it also requires really hearing what other people are trying to communicate, showing an accurate understanding, rather than quickly jumping in and giving advice or trying to fix things.

For many parents, the way I'm talking about communicating is so different that they say, "Well, it just doesn't seem natural to communicate that way." At just the right time while I was developing these ideas, I had read something that Gandhi had written, in which he said, "Don't mix up that which is habitual with that which is natural." Gandhi said that very often in our culture we've been trained to communicate and act in ways that are quite unnatural and yet have become habitual because we have been trained for various reasons to do it those ways. That quote certainly rang true to me in the way that I was trained to communicate with children. The way I was trained to communicate by judging rightness and wrongness, goodness and badness, and administering punishment was widely used and very easily became habitual for me as a parent. But I wouldn't say that just because something has become habitual, it is natural.

I learned that it is much more natural for people to connect in a loving, respectful way and to do things out of joy for one another, rather than using punishment and reward or blame and guilt as means of coercion. But such a transformation does require a good deal of consciousness and effort.

TRANSFORMING YOUR HABITUAL COMMUNICATION

I can recall one time when I was transforming myself from a habitually judgmental way of communicating with my children to the way that I am now advocating. On the day I'm thinking of, my oldest son and I were having a conflict, and it was taking me quite a while to communicate it in the way that I was choosing to, rather than the way that had become habitual. Almost everything that came into my mind was some coercive statement in the form of a judgment of him for saying what he had. So I had to stop, take a deep breath, and think of how to get more in touch with my needs and how to get more in touch with his needs. This was taking me a while, and he was getting frustrated because he had a friend waiting for him outside. He said, "Daddy, it's taking you so long to talk." And I said, "Let me tell you what I can say quickly: do it my way, or I'll kick your butt." He said, "Take your time, Dad. Take your time."

So yes, I would rather take my time and come from an energy that I choose in communicating with my children, rather than habitually responding in a way that I have been trained to do, when it's not really in harmony with my own values. Sadly, we often get much more reinforcement from those around us for behaving in a punitive, judgmental way than in a way that is respectful to our children.

I can recall one Thanksgiving dinner when I was doing my best to communicate with my youngest son in the way that I am advocating, and it was not easy because he was testing me to the limits. But I was taking my time, taking deep breaths, trying to understand what his needs were, trying to understand my own needs so I could express them in a respectful way. Another member of the family, observing my conversation with my son and having been trained in a different way of communicating, reached over at one point and whispered in my ear, "If that was my child, he'd be sorry for what he was saying."

I've talked to a lot of other parents who have had similar experiences—who, when they are trying to relate in more human ways with their own children, instead of getting support, often get criticized. People can often mistake what I'm talking about for permissiveness or not giving children the direction they need, instead of understanding that it's a different quality of direction. It's a direction that comes from two parties trusting each other, rather than from one party forcing his or her authority on the other.

One of the most unfortunate results of making our objective to get our children to do what we want—rather than having our objective be for all of us to get what we want—is that eventually our children will be hearing a demand in whatever we ask. And whenever people hear a demand, it's hard for them to keep focus on the value of whatever is being requested, because, as I said earlier, it threatens their autonomy, and that's a strong need that all people have. They want to be able to do something when they choose to do it and not because they are forced to do it. As soon as a person hears a demand, it's going to make any resolution that will get everybody's needs met much harder to come by.

"CHORE WARS"

For example, my children were given different tasks to do around the house. My youngest son, Brett, then twelve, was being asked to take the garbage out twice a week, so that it could be picked up by the garbage-removal people. This involved a simple act of removing the garbage from underneath the kitchen sink and taking it out on the front lawn where it could be picked up. This whole process could be done in five minutes. But it created a battle twice a week when the garbage was to go out.

How did this battle start? It usually started with my simply mentioning his name. I would say, "Brett." But of course, the way I said it, he could pick up that I was already angry because I was judging him as not doing what he should do. And even though I was saying his name loud enough so that the neighbors two blocks down could hear it, what does he do to keep escalating the war? He pretends that he doesn't hear me, even though he's in the next room. Well, what do I do? I get even angrier, of course, and I escalate further. I say the name even louder the second time, so that even he can't pretend that he doesn't hear me. And what does he do? He says, "What do you want?" I say, "The garbage isn't out." He says, "You're very perceptive." And I say, "Get it out." And he says, "I will, later." And I say, "You said that last time, but you didn't do it." And he says, "That doesn't mean I won't do it this time."

Look at all that energy going into the simple act of getting the garbage taken out. All the tension it created between us, all because at that time I had it in my mind that it was his job to do it, that he should do it, that it was necessary for him to learn responsibility. So, in other words, it was being presented to him as a demand.

People receive requests as demands if they think they will be punished or blamed if they don't do the task. When people have that idea, it takes all the joy out of doing anything.

One night I had a talk with Brett about this at a time when I was starting to get the point. I was starting to see how my thinking that I knew what was right, that my job as a parent was to get the children to behave, was destructive. So one night we had a talk about why the garbage wasn't going out, and by this time I was starting to learn how to listen better, to hear the feelings and needs that were behind his not doing what I asked. And I saw so clearly that he had a need to do things because he chose to do them and not to do them simply because he was being forced to do them.

So when I saw this, I said to him, "Brett, how do we get out of this? I know I really have been making demands in the past in the sense that when you didn't do things I wanted you to do, I would make judgments of you as being not a cooperative member of the family. So how do we get out of this history that we have, and how do we get to a place where we can do things for each other out of a different kind of energy?" And he came up with an idea that was very helpful. He said, "Dad, how about if I'm not sure if it's a request or a demand, I ask you, 'Is that a request or a demand?'" I said, "Hey, I like that idea. It would force me to really stop and look at my thinking and really see whether I am actually saying, 'Hey, I'd really like you to do this. It would meet my need, but if your needs are in conflict, I'd like to hear that, and let's figure out a way to get everybody's needs met.'"

I liked his suggestion to stop and really see what kind of assumptions were going on in me. And the next day before he went to school, we had three chances to test this out. Because three times in the morning I asked him to do something, and each time he looked at me and said, "Dad, is that a request or a demand?" And each time I looked inside, I saw that it was still a demand. I still had this thinking in me that he should do it, that it was the only reasonable thing for him to do. I was prepared to get progressively more coercive if he didn't do it. So it was helpful that he called this to my attention. Each time, I stopped, got in touch with my needs, tried to hear his needs, and I said to him, "OK, thank you. That helps. It was a demand, and now it's a request." And he could sense the difference in me. And each of those three times, he did it without question.

When people hear demands, it looks to them as though our caring and respect and love are conditional. It looks as though we are only going to care for them as people when they do what we want.

UNCONDITIONAL LOVE

I remember one time, years ago, when Brett was three years old, I was wondering whether I was communicating an unconditional quality of love to him and my other children. He just happened to be the one who came upon me at that time when I was thinking about this subject. As he came into the living room, I said, "Brett, why does Dad love you?" He looked at me and immediately said, "Because I make my potties in the toilet now?" I felt very sad the moment he said that, because it was so clear. How could he think differently? How differently I respond to my children when they do what I want than when they don't do what I want.

So I said to him, "Well, I do appreciate that, but that's not why I love you." And then he said, "Well, because I don't throw my food on the floor anymore?" He was referring to a little disagreement we'd had the night before when he was throwing some food on the floor. And I said, "Well, here again, I do appreciate it when you keep your food on your plate. But that's not why I love you."

Now he gets very serious and looks at me and says, "Well, why do you love me, Daddy?" And now I was wondering, why did I get into an abstract conversation about unconditional love with a three-year-old? How do you express this to someone his age? And I blurted out, "Well, I just love you because you're you." At the time, the immediate thought I had was, "That's pretty trite and vague," but he got it. He got the message. I just saw it in his face.

He brightened up, and he looked at me and said, "Oh, you just love me because I'm me, Daddy. You just love me because I'm me." The next two days it seemed like every ten minutes he was running over to me and pulling at my side and looking up and saying, "You just love me because I'm me, Daddy. You just love me because I'm me."

To communicate this quality of unconditional love, respect, and acceptance to other people doesn't mean that we have to like what they're doing. It doesn't mean we have to be permissive and give up our needs or values. What it requires is that we show people the same quality of respect when they don't do what we ask as when they do. After we have shown that quality of respect through empathy, through taking the time to understand why they didn't do what we would like, we can then pursue how we might influence them to willingly do what we ask. In some cases, when people are behaving in a serious way that threatens our needs or safety and there's not the time or ability to communicate about it, we may even use force. But unconditional love requires that no matter how people behave, they trust that they'll receive a certain quality of understanding from us.

PREPARING OUR CHILDREN

Of course, our children are often going to be in situations where they're not going to receive this unconditional acceptance and respect and love.

They're going to be in schools, perhaps, where the teachers are using a form of authority that's based on other ways of thinking—namely, that you have to earn respect and love, that you deserve to be punished or blamed if you don't behave in a certain way. So one of our tasks as parents is to show our children a way of staying human, even when they are being exposed to others who are using a form of coercion.

One of my happiest days as a parent was when my oldest son went off to a neighborhood school. He was twelve years old at the time. He had just finished six years in a school where I'd helped train the teachers, a school based on principles of Nonviolent Communication, where people were expected to do things not because of punishment or reward, but because they saw how it was contributing to their own and other people's well-being, where evaluation was in terms of needs and requests, not in terms of judgments. So this was going to be quite a different experience for him after six years in such a school—to go to the neighborhood school, which I'm sad to say wasn't functioning in a way that I would have liked.

Before he went off to this school, I had tried to provide him with some understanding of why teachers in this school might be communicating and behaving in a different way. I tried to provide him with some skills for handling that situation should it occur. When he came home from school the first day, I was delighted to find out how he had used what I had offered him.

I asked him, "Rick, how was the new school?" And he said, "Oh, it's OK, Dad. But boy, some of those teachers." I could see that he was distressed, and I said, "What happened?"

He said, "Dad, I wasn't even halfway in the door—really I was just walking in—when this man teacher saw me and came running over and screamed at me, 'My, my, look at the little girl.'" Now, what that teacher was reacting to was the fact that my son had long hair at the time, down to his shoulders. And this teacher had a way of thinking, apparently, where he thought he, as the authority, knew what was right—that there was a right way to wear hair, and that if people don't do things the right way, then you have to shame them or guilt them or punish them into doing it.

I felt sad to hear that my child would be greeted that way his first moment in the new school. And I said, "How did you handle it?" And he said, "Dad, I remembered what you said—that when you're in a place like that, never give them the power to make you submit or rebel." Well, I was delighted that he would remember that abstract principle at such a time.

And I told him I was glad that he remembered it, and I said, "How did you handle the situation?"

He said, "Dad, I also did what you suggested—that when people are talking to me that way, to try to hear what they're feeling and needing and not take it personally. Just to try to hear their feelings and needs."

I said, "Wow, am I glad that you thought to do that. What did you hear?"

He said, "Dad, it was pretty obvious. I heard that he was irritated and wanted me to cut my hair."

"Oh," I said. "How did that leave you feeling, to receive his message in that way?"

And he said, "Dad, I felt really sad for the man. He was bald and seemed to have a problem about hair."

THE "CAPTAIN" GAME

I had a very good experience with my children when they were three, four, and seven years old. I was then writing a book for teachers about how to create schools in harmony with the principles of Nonviolent Communication, in harmony with principles of mutual respect between teachers and students— to create schools that fostered the values of autonomy and interdependence. As part of the research I was doing in setting up these schools, I wanted to learn more about what kinds of choices we could trust children to make and to be able to turn these decisions over to children so that they were better able to develop their ability to make choices in their lives.

At this time, I thought a good way of learning more about this might be to play a game with my children that we called "Captain." Each day, I would appoint one of the children as captain. And when it was their turn as the captain, I would turn over many decisions that I would usually make to the captain. But I wouldn't give this decision to the children unless I was prepared to live with however they made their choices. As I said, my purpose in this game was to learn how children could make choices, how early they could make certain choices, and which ones might not be easy for them to make.

Here is an example of how this game went and what a good learning experience it was for me. Once I took the children with me to pick up some dry cleaning, and as I paid, the woman started to hand me three pieces of candy for the children. Immediately I saw a good opportunity to turn a decision over to the captain. As the woman handed me the candy, I said, "Uh, would you please give the candy to the captain?"

Well, she didn't know what I was talking about, but the captain did. Three-year-old Brett walked over, held out his hand, and she placed the candy in his hand. And then I said, "Captain, would you please choose what to do with this candy?"

Imagine this rough decision for this three-year-old captain. Here he is, three pieces of candy in his hand. He has a sister looking at him; he has a brother looking at him. How does he choose? Well, after a serious consideration, he gave one piece to his brother and one piece to his sister, and he ate the other himself.

When I first told that story to a group of parents, one of the parents said, "Well, yes, but that's because you had taught him that it was right to share." And I said to the parent, "Oh, I know that's not so, because a week before he was in a very similar situation, and he ate all three pieces of candy. Can you guess what happened to him the next day? He learned the next day that if we don't take other people's needs into consideration, our own needs can never really be met. He really got a quick lesson on interdependence. It was thrilling for me to see how quickly children saw this when they really had choices to make—that we can never really take care of ourselves without showing equal concern for the needs of others."

As I said, it's not easy for parents to let go of the concept of punishment. It's deeply ingrained in many parents that punishment is a necessity. And they can't imagine what else can be done when children are behaving in ways that might be harmful to themselves and other people. They can't conceive of other options besides permissiveness, just letting it go, or using some kind of punitive action.

THE USE OF FORCE

I have found it very important to get across to such parents the concept of the protective use of force and to get them to see the difference between the protective use of force and the punitive use of force. When might we sometimes have to use a form of force with our children?

The conditions calling for this type of force would be when there isn't time to communicate and children's behavior might be injurious to themselves or other people. Or it could be that someone isn't willing to talk. So if people aren't willing to talk, or there isn't time to talk, and meanwhile they are behaving in a way that is in conflict with one of our needs—such as a need to protect others—we might have to use force. But now we have to see the difference between the protective and the punitive use of force. One way that these two uses of force differ is in the thinking of the person who is engaging in the force.

In the punitive use of force, the person using such force has made a moralistic judgment of others, a judgment that implies some kind of wrongness that is deserving of punishment. Those others deserve to suffer for what they've done. That's the whole idea of punishment. It comes out of these ideas that human beings are basically sinful, evil creatures, and the corrective process is to make them penitent. We have to get them to see how terrible they are for doing what they're doing, and the way we make them penitent is to use some form of punishment to make them suffer. Sometimes this can be a physical punishment in the form of spanking, or it could be a psychological punishment in the form of trying to make them hate themselves through making them feel guilty or ashamed.

The thinking behind the protective use of force is radically different. There is no consciousness that the other person is bad or deserving of punishment. Our consciousness is fully focused on our needs. We are conscious of what need of ours is in danger, but we are not in any way implying badness or wrongness to the child.

This kind of thinking is one significant difference between the protective use of force and the punitive use of force. And this thinking is closely related to a second difference: the intent. In the punitive use of force, it is our intent to create pain and suffering for the other person, to make them sorry for what they did. In the protective use of force, our intent is only to protect. We protect our needs, and then later we'll have the communication necessary to educate the person. But at the moment it may be necessary to use the force to protect.

An example of this would be how when my children were young and we lived on a busy street, they seemed to be fascinated with what was going on across the street, but they hadn't yet learned the dangers of what can happen if you just dart out in the street. I was certain that if we could talk long enough about this I could educate them, but in the meantime I was afraid that they could be killed. So here was a case for the protective use of force—there not being the time to communicate about this before something serious could happen. So what I said to them was, "If I see you running in the street, I'm going to put you in the backyard where I don't have to worry about you getting hit by a car." Not long after I said that, one of them forgot and started to run in the street. I picked him up, carried him into the yard, and put him there. It was not as a punishment—there was plenty to do in the yard; we had swings and a slide. I wasn't trying to make him suffer. I was only wanting to control the environment to meet my need for safety.

Now many parents say, "Well, isn't the child likely to see that as a punishment?" Well, if it has been intended as a punishment in the past, if the child has had a lot of experience seeing force as punitive, then yes, that child could still see it as a punishment. The main thing, though, is that we, the parents, are conscious of this difference, and that if we use force we're certain that it is to protect and not to punish.

One way of remembering the purpose of the protective use of force is to see the difference between controlling the child and controlling the environment. In punishment, we're trying to control children by making them feel bad about what they've done, to create an internal shame, guilt, or fear for what they have done. In the protective use of force, however, our intent is not to control the child; it's to control the environment, to protect our needs until such time as we can have the quality of communication with the child that's really necessary. It's somewhat like putting screens on our house to protect us from being bitten by mosquitoes. It's a protective use of force. We control the environment to prevent things happening that we don't want to happen.

SUPPORTIVE COMMUNITIES

The way of parenting that I'm advocating here is quite different from how most people are parenting. It's going to be difficult to consider radically different options in a world where punishment is so prevalent and where you are likely to be misinterpreted if you don't use punishment and other coercive forms of parental behavior. It can really help to be part of a supportive community that understands the concept of parenting I'm talking about, a community that gives the support to continue to do this in a world that doesn't often support it.

I know that I was always much better able to stay with what I'm now talking about if I was getting a lot of empathy from a supportive community—empathy for how hard it can be to be a parent at times and for how easy it is to fall into old patterns. When I had other parents trying to connect with their children as I was, it was very supportive to be able to talk to them—to hear their frustrations, to have them hear mine. And I noticed that the more that I was part of such a community, the better able I was to stay with this process with my children, even under difficult conditions.

One of the rewarding things that happened—something that was very encouraging and enriching—was a message I received from my daughter when she was very small. It was on a Sunday morning, the only time of the week when I could relax, a very precious time for me. On this particular Sunday morning, a couple called me and asked if I would be willing to see them in counseling. They had a crisis in their relationship and wanted me to work with them. I agreed to do this without really looking inside myself, seeing what my own needs were and how I was resenting their intrusion on my time to relax. While I had them in the living room, counseling them, the doorbell rang and the police brought in a young woman for me to see. I had also been seeing her in counseling, and they had found her down on the railroad tracks. That was her way of letting me know she wanted to see me. She was too shy to call up and ask for another appointment. This was her way—sitting on the railroad tracks—of letting me know she was in distress. She knew the train schedule better than anyone in town, so she knew the police would pick her up before the train got her.

The police left, and I had this young woman in the kitchen crying and the couple in the living room. I was going back and forth trying to lovingly counsel both. While I was walking from one room to the other looking at my watch, hoping I would still have time afterward for some time to myself, the three children upstairs started fighting. So I bounded up the stairs, and I found something fascinating. I might write this up in a scientific paper some day: the effect of altitude on maniac behavior. Because you see, downstairs I was a very loving person, giving love to this couple, giving love to the young woman in the other room, but one flight of stairs up and I was a maniac.

I said to my children, "What's the matter with you? Can't you see that I have hurting people downstairs? Now get in your rooms!" And each went in their rooms and each slammed the door just loud enough that I couldn't prove it was a slam. With the first slam, I got outraged; with the second slam, I got even more outraged. But fortunately, with the third slam, I don't know why, it helped me see the humor in the situation. How easy it was for me to be loving of these people downstairs, but how quickly I could get brutal with my own family upstairs.

I took a deep breath, and I went into my oldest son's room. I told him I was sad that I was taking out some feelings on him, feelings that I was afraid I really had for the people downstairs. He understood; he just said, "It's OK, Dad. Nothing big." I went in my youngest son's room and got a pretty similar response from him. When I went in my daughter's room and told her that I felt sad at the way I had talked to her, she came over and put her head on my shoulder and said, "It's OK, Daddy. Nobody's perfect."

What a precious message to hear. Yes, my children appreciate my efforts to relate to them in a caring way, in a compassionate way, an empathic way. But how relieving it is that they can understand my humanness and how difficult it can sometimes be.

So in closing, I offer you that reassuring advice given to me by my daughter: nobody's perfect. Remember that anything that's worth doing is worth doing poorly. And the job of parenting, of course, is extremely worth doing, but we're going to do it poorly at times. If we're going to be brutal with ourselves when we're not perfect parents, our children are going to suffer for that.

I often tell the parents that I'm working with that hell is having children and thinking there's such a thing as a good parent. If every time we're less than perfect we're going to blame ourselves and attack ourselves, our children are not going to benefit from that. So the goal I would suggest is not to be perfect parents; it's to become progressively less stupid parents—by learning from each time that we're not able to give our children the quality of understanding that they need, that we're not able to express ourselves honestly. In my experience, each of these times usually means that we're not getting the emotional support we need as parents in order to give our children what they need.

We can only really give in a loving way to the degree that we are receiving similar love and understanding. So that's why I strongly recommend that we look at how we might create a supportive community for ourselves among our friends and others who can give us the understanding we need to be present to our children in a way that will be good for them and good for us.

I hope that something I've said here has helped you grow closer to becoming the parent you would like to be.

6

PRACTICAL SPIRITUALITY

Reflections on the Spiritual Basis
of Nonviolent Communication

Whenever I speak about my deeply held beliefs—spirituality, concepts of God, views of love—two themes always emerge: (1) the greatest joy springs from connecting to life by contributing to our own and others' well-being, and (2) spirituality and love are more about what we do than what we feel.

People frequently ask me how I got to that place, how I relate to the religious beliefs of others, and what my views mean for the practice of NVC. What follows are excerpts of my unscripted verbal responses to queries from media interviewers and workshop participants on the subject of spirituality, the concept of the Divine, the spiritual basis of NVC, and applying NVC values to social change.

Q: HOW DO WE CONNECT WITH THE DIVINE THROUGH NONVIOLENT COMMUNICATION?

A: I think it is important that people see that spirituality is at the base of Nonviolent Communication and that they learn the mechanics of the NVC process with that in mind. It's really a spiritual practice that I am trying to show as a way of life. Even though we don't make a point of mentioning this, people get seduced by the practice. Even if they practice NVC as a mechanical technique, they start to experience things between themselves and other people that they weren't able to experience before. So eventually they come to the spirituality of the process. They begin to see that it's more than a communication process and realize it's really an attempt to manifest our spirituality. I have tried to integrate spirituality into the practice of NVC in a way that meets my need not to destroy the beauty of it through abstract philosophizing.

The kind of world I'd like to live in will require some rather significant social changes, but the changes that I'd like to see happen probably won't happen unless the people working toward them are coming out of a different spirituality than what has led to the predicaments we're in now. So our training is designed to help people make sure that the spirituality that's guiding them is one of their own choosing and not one they've internalized from the culture, and that they proceed in creating social change out of that spirituality.

Q: WHAT DOES "GOD" MEAN TO YOU?

A: I need a way to think of God that works for me—other words or ways to look at this beauty, this powerful energy. And so my name for God is *Beloved Divine Energy*. For a while it was just *Divine Energy*. But then I was reading some of the Eastern religions and Eastern poets, and I loved how they had this personal, loving connection with this energy. And I found that it added to my life to call it Beloved Divine Energy. To me this Beloved Divine Energy is life, connection to life.

Q: WHAT IS YOUR FAVORITE WAY OF KNOWING BELOVED DIVINE ENERGY?

A: It is how I connect with human beings. I know Beloved Divine Energy by connecting with human beings in a certain way. I not only see Divine Energy, but I also taste Divine Energy, I feel Divine Energy, and I am Divine Energy. I'm connected with Beloved Divine Energy when I connect with human beings in this way. Then God is very alive for me.

Q: WHAT RELIGIOUS BELIEFS, TEACHINGS, OR WRITINGS HAVE HAD THE GREATEST INFLUENCE ON YOU?

A: It's hard for me to say which of the various religions on the planet have had the most impact on me. Probably Buddhism as much as any. I like so much of what I understand the Buddha or the people who quoted the Buddha to be saying. For example, the Buddha makes it very clear: don't get addicted to your strategies, your requests, or your desires. That's a very important part of our training: to not mix real human needs with the way we've been educated to get those needs met. So be careful to not get your strategies mixed up with your needs. We don't need a new car, for example. Some people may choose a new car as a strategy for meeting a need for reliability or peace of mind, but you've got to watch out, because society can trick you into thinking it's the new car that you really need. This part of our training is very much in harmony with my understanding of the Buddha.

Almost all the religions and mythologies I've studied say a very similar message, one that Joseph Campbell, the mythologist, summarizes in some of his work: *don't do anything that isn't play.* And what they mean by play is willingly contributing to life. So don't do anything to avoid punishment, don't do anything for rewards, don't do anything out of guilt, shame, and the vicious concepts of duty and obligation. What you do will be play when you can see how it enriches life. I get that message from my understanding not only of the Buddha, but also from what I have learned about Islam, Christianity, and Judaism. I think it's a natural language. Do that which contributes to life.

Q: DOESN'T THE INFLUENCE OF RELIGION AND SPIRITUALITY PROMOTE PASSIVITY, OR AN "OPIATE OF THE MASSES" EFFECT?

A: I'm very worried about any spirituality that allows us to just sit comfortably in the world and say, "But I am helping the world. The energy alone coming from me is going to create social change." Rather, I trust a spirituality that leads people to go forward and transform the world, that doesn't just sit there with this beautiful image of radiating energy. I want to see that energy reflected in people's actions as they go out and make things happen. It's something you do, a practical spirituality.

Q: SO NONVIOLENT COMMUNICATION EVOLVED IN PART FROM SPIRITUAL ORIGINS?

A: Nonviolent Communication evolved from my attempt to get conscious about Beloved Divine Energy and how to connect with it. I was dissatisfied with input from my chosen field of clinical psychology, because it was and is pathology-based and I didn't like its language. It didn't give me a view of the beauty of human beings. So, after I got my degree, I decided to go more in the direction of Carl Rogers and Abraham Maslow.

I decided to ask myself the scary questions, "What are we, and what are we meant to be?" I found that there was very little written about this in psychology. So I took a crash course in comparative religion, because I saw that it dealt more with this question. And this word *love* kept coming up in each of them.

I used to hear the word *love* as many people used it—in a religious sense, like, "You should love everybody." I used to get really annoyed at the word *love*. "Oh yeah, I'm supposed to love Hitler?" I didn't know the words *New Age bullshit,* but I used what was my equivalent then. I tried to understand better what love means because I could see it had so much meaning for so many millions of people in all these religions. What is it, and how do you "do" this "love"?

Nonviolent Communication really came out of my attempt to understand this concept of love and how to manifest it, how to do it. I came to the conclusion that it was not just something we feel, but it is something we manifest, something we do, something we have. And what is this manifestation? It is giving of ourselves in a certain way.

Q: WHAT DO YOU MEAN BY "GIVING OF OURSELVES"?

A: To me, giving of ourselves means an honest expression of what's alive in us in this moment. It intrigues me that in every culture people ask upon greeting each other, "How are you?" In English they say it this way: *How are you?* In Spanish, *¿Cómo estás?* French is *Comment allez-vous?* German is *Wie Geht es Dir?* We say it as a social ritual, but it's a very important question, because if we're to live in peace and harmony, if we're to enjoy contributing to one another's well-being, we need to know what's alive in one another. It's such an important question. What a gift it is to be able to know at any given moment what is alive in someone.

To give a gift of one's self is a manifestation of love. It's a gift when you reveal yourself nakedly and honestly, at any given moment, for no other purpose than to reveal what's alive in you. Not to blame, criticize, or punish. Just "Here I am, and here is what I would like." This is my vulnerability at this moment. To me, that is a way of manifesting love.

The other way we give of ourselves is through how we receive another person's message. To receive it empathically, connecting with what's alive in that person, making no judgment. Just to hear what is alive in the other person and what that person would like.

So Nonviolent Communication is just a manifestation of what I understand love to be. In that way it's similar to the Judeo-Christian concepts of "Love your neighbor as yourself" and "Judge not lest you be judged."

Q: NONVIOLENT COMMUNICATION CAME OUT OF YOUR DESIRE TO MANIFEST LOVE?

A: I was also helped by empirical research in psychology that defined the characteristics of healthy relationships and by studying people who were living manifestations of loving people. Out of these sources, I pulled together a process that helped me connect with people in what I could understand is a loving way.

And then I saw what happened when I did connect with people in this way. This beauty, this power connected me with an energy that I choose to call Beloved Divine Energy. So Nonviolent Communication helps me stay connected with that beautiful Divine Energy within myself and to connect with it in others. And certainly when I connect that Divine Energy within myself with the Divine Energy in others, what happens is the closest thing to knowing what it is to be connected to God.

It helps to remember that a key purpose of Nonviolent Communication is to connect with other people—and thus with Divine Energy—in a way that enables compassionate giving to take place. It's giving that comes from the heart willingly, where we are giving service to ourselves and others not out of duty or obligation; not out of fear of punishment or hope for a reward; not out of guilt or shame, but for what I consider is our nature—our nature to enjoy giving to one another. In Nonviolent Communication we strive to connect with one another in a way that allows our nature to come forward.

When I say that I think it's our nature to enjoy giving, some people may wonder whether I'm a little bit naive and unaware of all the violence in the world. How can I think it's our nature to enjoy compassionate giving with what's happening? Unfortunately, I see the violence. I work in places like Rwanda, Israel, Palestine and Sri Lanka, and I'm well aware of it all. But I don't think that's our nature.

In every place I work, I ask people the following: "Think of something you've done within the past twenty-four hours that in some way has contributed to making life more wonderful for somebody." And when they've recalled something, I then say, "Now, how do you feel when you are aware of how that act contributed to making life more wonderful for somebody?" And everybody is smiling. When we are aware of the power we have to enrich life, it feels good—it feels good to serve life.

And then I ask people, "Can anybody think of anything that's more fulfilling in life than to use our efforts this way?" And I've asked that question all over our planet, and everyone seems in agreement. There's nothing that is better, nothing that feels better; nothing is more enjoyable than using our efforts in the service of life, contributing to one another's well-being.

Q: HOW DO YOU PREVENT EGO FROM INTERFERING WITH YOUR CONNECTION WITH GOD?

A: By seeing ego as very closely tied to the way my culture has trained me to think and trained me to communicate. And how the culture has trained me to meet my needs in certain ways, to get my needs mixed up with the strategies I might use to meet my needs. So I try to remain conscious of these three ways that the culture has programmed me to do things that really aren't in my best interest, to function more from ego than from my connection with Divine Energy. I have tried to learn ways to train myself to become conscious of this culturally learned thinking, and I've incorporated these into Nonviolent Communication.

Q: THEN YOU BELIEVE THAT THE LANGUAGE OF OUR CULTURE PREVENTS US FROM KNOWING OUR DIVINE ENERGY MORE INTIMATELY?

A: Oh yes, definitely. I think our language makes it really hard, especially the language given to us by the cultural training most of us seem to have gone through and the associations the word *God* brings up for many people. Judgmental, or right/wrong thinking, is one of the hardest things I've found to overcome in teaching Nonviolent Communication over the years. The people I work with have all gone to schools and churches, and if they like Nonviolent Communication it's very easy for them to say it's the "right way" to communicate. It's very easy to think that Nonviolent Communication is the goal.

I've altered a Buddhist parable that relates to this question. Imagine a beautiful, whole, and sacred place. And imagine that you could really know God when you are in that place. But let's say that there is a river between you and that place, and you'd like to get to that place but you have to get over this river to do it. So you get a raft, and this raft is a really handy tool to get you across the river. Once you're across the river, you can walk the rest of the several miles to this beautiful place. But the Buddhist parable ends by saying that "one is a fool who continues on to the sacred place carrying the raft on their back."

Nonviolent Communication is a tool to get me over my cultural training, so I can get to the place. NVC is not the place. If we get addicted to the raft, attached to the raft, it makes it harder to get to the place. People just learning the process of Nonviolent Communication sometimes forget all about the place. If they get too locked into the raft, the process becomes mechanical.

Nonviolent Communication is one of the most powerful tools that I've found for connecting with people in a way that helps us get connected to the Divine, where what we do toward one another comes out of Divine Energy. That's the place I want to get to.

Q: IS THIS THE SPIRITUAL BASIS OF NONVIOLENT COMMUNICATION?

A: The spiritual basis for me is that I'm trying to connect with the Divine Energy in others and connect them with the Divine in me, because I believe that when we are really connected with that divinity within one another and ourselves, we can enjoy contributing to one another's well-being more than anything else. So for me, if we're connected with the Divine in others and ourselves, we are going to enjoy what happens, and that's the spiritual basis. In this place, violence is impossible.

Q: IS THIS LACK OF CONNECTION TO DIVINE ENERGY RESPONSIBLE FOR VIOLENCE IN THE WORLD?

A: I would say it this way: I think we have been given the gift of choice to create the world of our choosing. And we've been given this great and abundant world for creating a world of joy and nurturing. To me, violence in the world comes about when we get alienated or disconnected from this Divine Energy.

How do we get connected when we are educated to be disconnected? I believe it's our cultural conditioning and education that disconnects us from God—especially our education *about* God. And I believe that *violence comes because of how we were educated, not because of our nature.* According to theologian Walter Wink, we have been edu-cated for about eight thousand years in a way that makes violence enjoyable, that gets us disconnected from our compassionate nature.

And why were we educated this way? That's a long story, and I won't go into it here, except to say that it started with myths that began to develop long ago about human nature—myths that humans were basically evil, selfish, and that the good life is all about heroic forces crushing evil forces. Wink wrote about how domination cultures use certain teachings about God to maintain oppression. That's why priests and kings have often been closely related. The kings needed the priests to justify the oppression, to interpret the holy books in ways that justi-fied punishment, domination, and so forth.

So we've been living under a destructive mythology for a long time, and that destructive mythology requires a certain language. It requires a language that dehumanizes people, turns them into objects. We have learned to think in terms of moralistic judgments of one another. We have words in our consciousness like *right, wrong, good, bad, selfish, unselfish, terrorists, freedom fighters.* And connected to these is the concept of justice based on *deserve*—that if you do one of these bad things, you deserve to be punished. If you do the good things, then you deserve to be rewarded.

Unfortunately, for about eight thousand years we have been sub-jected to that consciousness. I think that's the core of violence on our planet: faulty education. The process of Nonviolent Communication is an integration of thought, language, and communication that I think brings us closer to our nature. It helps us to connect with one another so that we come back to what is really the fun way to live, which is contributing to one another's well-being.

Q: HOW DO WE OVERCOME THIS CONDITIONING?

A: I'm often in between people in a lot of pain. I remember working with twenty Serbians and twenty Croatians. Some of the people there had family members killed by the other side, and they all had generations of poison pumped into their heads about the other side. They spent three days expressing their rage and pain to one another. Fortunately, we were there for seven days.

One word I haven't used yet in speaking about the power of NVC is the word *inevitability.* So many times I have seen that no matter what has happened, if people connect in this certain way, it is inevitable that they will end up enjoying giving to one another. It is *inevitable*. For me, my work is like watching a magic show. It's too beautiful for words.

But sometimes this Divine Energy doesn't work as fast as I think it should. I remember sitting there in the middle of all this rage and pain and thinking, "Divine Energy, if you can heal all this stuff why are you taking so long, why are you putting these people through this?" And the Energy spoke to me, and it said, "You just do what you can to connect. Bring your energy in. Connect and help the other people connect, and let me take care of the rest." But even though that was going on in one part of my brain, I knew joy was inevitable if we could just keep getting connected to our own and one another's Divine Energy.

And it happened. It happened with great beauty. The last day everybody was talking about joy. And many of them said, "You know, I thought I was never going to feel joy again after what we've been through." This was the theme on everybody's lips. That evening, the twenty Serbians and twenty Croatians, who seven days earlier had only unimaginable pain in relation to one another, danced one another's dances, sang one another's songs, and celebrated the joy of life together.

Q: WE GAIN THIS CONNECTION TO EACH OTHER BY KNOWING GOD?

A: I want to stay away from intellectualizing about God. If by "knowing God," we mean this intimate connection with Beloved Divine Energy, then we gain every second as experiencing heaven.

The heaven I gain from knowing God is this inevitability, to know it is inevitable—that, no matter what the hell is going on, if we get to this level of connection with one another, if we get in touch with one another's Divine Energy, it's inevitable that we will enjoy giving, and we'll give back to life. I've been through such ugly stuff with people that I don't get worried about it anymore. It's inevitable. If we get that quality of connection, we'll like where it gets us.

It amazes me how effective it is. I could tell you similar examples between the extremist Israelis, both politically and religiously, and the same on the Palestinian side, and between the Hutus and the Tutsis, and between Christian and Muslim tribes in Nigeria. With all of them, it amazes me how easy it is to bring about this reconciliation and healing.

Once again, all we have to do is get both sides connected to the other person's needs. To me, the needs are the quickest, closest way of getting in connection with that Divine Energy. Everyone has the same needs. The needs come because we're alive.

Q: EXACTLY HOW DO WE GAIN THIS CONNECTION TO DIVINE ENERGY AND TO OTHER PEOPLE?

A: There are two basic parts to the process. The first is learning how to express ourselves in a language of life. The other half of the process is how we respond to other people's messages. In Nonviolent Communication, we try to keep our attention focused by answering two critical questions: *What's alive in us?* and *What can we do to make life more wonderful?*

The first question, "What's alive in me; what's alive in you?" is a question that all over the planet people ask themselves when they get together: "How are you?"

Sadly, even though most people ask the question, very few people really know how to answer it very well, because we haven't been educated in a language of life. We've not really been taught to answer the question. We ask it, yes, but we don't know how to answer it. Nonviolent Communication, as we'll see, suggests how we can let people know what's alive in us. It shows us how to connect with what's alive in other people, even if they don't have words for saying it.

Q: HOW DO WE EXPRESS WHAT'S ALIVE IN US?

A: Expressing what's alive in us requires literacy on three levels. First of all, it requires being able to answer the question "What's alive in you?" without mixing in any evaluation. That's what I call an *observation*. What do people do that we either like or don't like? That's important information to communicate. To tell people what's alive in us, we need to tell the other person what they're doing that is supporting life in us *and* what they're doing that isn't supporting life in us. But it's very important to learn how to say that to people without mixing in any evaluation. So this is the first step in trying to tell people what's alive in us: to be able to call their attention—concretely, specifically—to what the person's doing that we like or don't like and not mix in any evaluation.

With an observation in mind of what this person does, if we're to use Nonviolent Communication, we want to be honest with that person about it. But it's an honesty of a different kind from telling people what's wrong with them—honesty from the heart, not honesty that implies wrongness. We want to go inside and tell the person what's alive in us when this person does this. And this involves the other two forms of literacy we need: feeling literacy and need literacy. *To say clearly what's alive in us at any given moment, we have to be clear about what we feel and what we need.* So let's start with the feelings.

We have *feelings* every moment. The problem is that we haven't learned how to be conscious of what's alive in us. Our consciousness has been directed to make us look outward to what authority thinks we are. There are different ways we might express our feelings, depending on what culture we grow up in, but it is important to have a vocabulary of feelings that really does describe what's alive in us and that doesn't include interpretations of other people. We don't want to use words like *misunderstood,* because that's not really a feeling; that's more how we are analyzing whether the other person has understood us. If we think somebody has misunderstood us, sometimes we can be angry, frustrated—it could be many different things. Likewise, we don't want to use words like *manipulated* or *criticized.* They're not what we call feelings in our training. Sadly, very few people have much of a feeling vocabulary, and I see the cost of that very often in my work.

Is it really an expression of what's alive in you, your feelings? Make sure that it's not a thought diagnosis of others. Go into your heart. How do you feel when others do what they do?

Editor's note: For complete feelings and needs vocabularies, please see Nonviolent Communication: A Language of Life *by Marshall B. Rosenberg, PhD.*

Q: DO YOU SUGGEST THAT SIMPLY TELLING PEOPLE HOW WE FEEL IS ALL THAT'S NEEDED?

A: No, feelings can be used in a destructive way if we try to imply that other people's behavior is the cause of our feelings. *The cause of our feelings is our needs, not other people's behavior.* And this is the third component of expressing what's alive in us: *needs.* Getting connected to what's alive in us is getting connected to our own Divine Energy.

When I was six years old, we used to say this when somebody would call us a name: "Sticks and stones can break my bones, but names will never hurt me." We were aware then that *it's not what other people do that can hurt you; it's how you take it.* But we were educated in guilt-inducing ways by authorities, teachers, and parents, who used guilt to mobilize us to do what they wanted. They would express feelings this way: "It hurts me when you don't clean up your room." "You make me angry when you hit your brother." We've been educated by people who tried to make us feel responsible for their feelings so we would feel guilty. Feelings are important, but we don't want to use them in that way. We don't want to use them in a guilt-inducing manner. It's very important that when we do express our feelings, we follow our feelings with a statement that makes it clear that *the cause of our feelings is our needs.*

Q: WHAT PREVENTS PEOPLE FROM JUST SAYING WHAT THEY NEED?

A: Just as it's difficult for many people to develop a literacy of feelings, it's also very difficult for them to develop a literacy of needs. Many people, in fact, have very negative associations with needs. They associate needs with being needy, dependent, selfish—and again, I think that comes from our history of educating people to fit well into domination structures so that they are obedient and submissive to authority. People do not make good slaves when they're in touch with their needs. I went to schools for twenty-one years, and I can't recall ever being asked what my needs were. And my education didn't focus on helping me be more alive, more in touch with myself and others. It was oriented toward rewarding me for getting right answers as defined by authorities. Look at the words that you are using to describe your needs. Needs do not contain any reference to specific people taking specific actions. Needs are universal. All human beings have the same needs.

When we can connect at the need level, when we see one another's humanness, it's amazing how conflicts that seem unsolvable become solvable. I do a lot of work with people in conflict—husbands and wives, parents and children, tribes of people. Many of these people think they have a conflict that can't be resolved. And it's been amazing to me, over the years that I've been doing conflict resolution and mediation work, what happens when you can get people over their diagnoses of one another, get them connected at the need level to what's going on in one another—how conflicts that appear impossible to resolve seem like they almost resolve themselves.

Q: SO, WHAT'S NEXT AFTER FEELINGS AND NEEDS?

A: We have expressed the three pieces of information that are necessary to answer the question "What's alive in us?" We've expressed what we're observing, what we're feeling, and the needs of ours that are connected to our feelings.

This brings us to the *second question,* which is related to the first: "What can we do to make life more wonderful?" What can you do to make life more wonderful for me? What can I do to make life more wonderful for you? That's the other half of connecting with the Divine Energy in us: how to make empathic connection with what's alive in the other person in order to make life more wonderful for the other person.

Let me tell you what I mean by empathic connection. Empathy, of course, is a special kind of understanding. It's not an understanding of the head, where we just mentally understand what another person says. It's something far deeper and more precious than that. Empathic connection is an understanding of the heart, where we see the beauty in the other person, the Divine Energy in the other person, the life that's alive in that person. We connect with it. We don't mentally understand it; we connect with it.

It doesn't mean we have to feel the same feelings as the other person. That's sympathy—when we feel sad, maybe because another person is upset. It doesn't mean that we have to have the same feelings; it means that we are *with* the other person.

This quality of understanding requires one of the most precious gifts one human being can give to another: our presence in the moment. If we're mentally trying to understand other people, then we're not present with them in this moment. We're sitting there analyzing them, but we're not with them. So empathic connection involves *connecting with what is alive in the other person at this moment.*

Q: WHAT KEEPS US FROM CONNECTING TO THE LIFE IN ONE ANOTHER AS YOU SUGGEST?

A: We have been educated to think that there is something wrong with us. I want to suggest that you should never, never, never hear what other people think about you. I predict you'll live longer, and you'll enjoy life more if you never hear what people think about you. Never take it personally. The recommendation I have is to learn to connect empathically with any message coming at us from other people. And Nonviolent Communication shows us a way of doing that. It shows us a way of seeing the beauty in the other person in any given moment, regardless of their behavior or their language. It requires connecting with the other person's feelings and needs at this moment, with what's alive in them. And when we do that, we're going to hear the other person singing a very beautiful song.

I was working with some twelve year olds in a school in the state of Washington, showing them how to make empathic connections with people. And they wanted me to show them how they could deal with parents and teachers. They were afraid of what they would get back if they opened up and revealed what was alive in them. One of the students said, "Marshall, I was honest with one of my teachers. I said I didn't understand, and I asked her to explain it again. And the teacher said, 'Don't you listen? I've explained it twice already.'"

Another young man said, "I asked my dad yesterday for something. I tried to express my needs to him, and he said, 'You're the most selfish child in the family.'"

They were very eager to have me show them how to empathically connect with the people in their lives who use language like that, because they only knew how to take it personally, to think that there was something wrong with them. I showed the students that if you learn how to connect empathically with other people, you will hear that they are always singing a beautiful song expressing their needs. That's what you will hear behind every message coming at you from another human being if you connect to the Divine Energy in that person at that moment.

Q: CAN YOU GIVE AN EXAMPLE OF HOW TO MAKE AN EMPATHIC CONNECTION WITH SOMEONE?

A: You start by telling them what they've done, how you feel, what needs of yours aren't getting met. Now, what can be done to make life more wonderful? This takes the form of a clear request. We need to request what we would like them to do to make life more wonderful for us. We've told them the pain we feel in relationship to what their behavior is, what needs of ours aren't getting met. Now we're going to say what we would like them to do to make life more wonderful for us.

Nonviolent Communication suggests that we make our request using positive action language. Let me explain what I mean: *positive* in the sense of what you want them to do in contrast to what you don't want or what you want them to stop doing. We get to a different place with people when we are clear about what we want, rather than just telling them what we don't want.

A good example of that was a teacher recently in a workshop who said, "Oh, Marshall, you've just helped me understand what happened to me yesterday."

I said, "What was that?"

She said, "There was this boy tapping on his book while I was talking to the class. And I said, 'Would you please stop tapping on your book?' So he started to tap on his desk."

You see, telling people what we don't want is far different from telling them what we do want. When we try to get somebody to stop something, it makes punishment look like an effective strategy. But if we ask ourselves two questions, we would never use punishment again. We would never use it with children; we would create a judicial system, a correctional system, that does not punish criminals for what they've done; and we wouldn't try to punish other nations for what they're doing to us. Punishment is a losing game.

As I have mentioned before, we would see that if only we asked these two questions. Question number one: What do we want the other person to do? See, it's not what we don't want. *What do we want the person to do?*

Again, if we ask only that question, it can still make punishment seem like it works sometimes, because we can probably recall times when we've used punishment and were successful at getting somebody to do what we wanted. But, if we add a second question, we see that punishment never works. And what is the second question? *What do we want their reasons to be for doing what we want them to do?*

The purpose of Nonviolent Communication is to create connections so people do things for one another out of compassion, out of connection to Divine Energy, to serve life—not out of fear of punishment, not out of hope for rewards, but because of the natural joy we feel in contributing to one another's well-being. So when we make our request, we want to do it in the positive—what we *do* want.

Q: HOW DO YOU EXPRESS YOUR NEEDS AS REQUESTS WITHOUT SOUNDING LIKE YOU'RE DEMANDING SOMETHING?

A: We do want to make clear, assertive requests, but we want other people to know that these are requests and not demands. Now, what's the difference? First, you can't tell the difference by how nicely it is asked. So if we do say to someone living with us, "I would like you to hang up your clothes when you're finished with them," is that a request or a demand? We don't know yet. You can never tell whether something is a request or a demand by how nicely it is asked or how clear it is. What determines the difference between a request and a demand is how we treat people when they don't do as we've asked. That's what tells people whether we make requests or demands.

Now, what happens when people hear demands? Well, it's pretty obvious with some people when they've heard your request as a demand. One time I asked my youngest son, "Would you please hang your coat up in the closet?" And he said, "Who was your slave before I was born?" OK, well, it's easy to be around such a person, because if they hear your request as a demand, you know it right away. But other people, when they hear a request as a demand, respond quite differently. They'll say, "OK," but then they don't do it. Or the worst case is when the person hears the demand, they say, "OK," and they do it. But they do it because they heard a demand. They were afraid of what would happen to them if they didn't. Anytime somebody does what we ask out of guilt, shame, duty, obligation, fear of punishment, anything that people do for us out of that energy, we're going to pay for it. We want people to do for us only when they're connected to that kind of Divine Energy that exists in all of us. Divine Energy is manifest to me by the joy we feel in giving to one another. We're not doing it to avoid punishment, guilt, and all of those things.

Q: WHAT ABOUT DISCIPLINE? WHAT YOU'RE SUGGESTING SOUNDS LIKE JUST BEING PERMISSIVE.

A: Some people cannot believe that you can have order in the house and the government unless you force people to do things, unless you make demands. For example, one mother I was working with said, "But, Marshall, that's all very well and good, to hope that people are going to respond out of Divine Energy, but what about a child? I mean, a child has to first learn what they *have to* do, what they *should* do." This mother was using two of the words, or concepts, that I think are the most destructive concepts on the planet today: *have to* and *should*. She didn't trust that there's Divine Energy in children, as well as in adults, so that they can do things not because they fear they're going to be punished, but because they see the joy that comes from contributing to other people's well-being.

I said to the mother, "I hope today I can show you other ways of presenting things to your children so that it's more of a request.

They see your needs. They don't do it because they think they have to. They see the choice, and they respond out of this Divine Energy within themselves."

She says, "I do all kinds of things every day that I hate to do, but there are just some things you *have to* do."

I said, "Could you give me an example?"

She said, "OK. Here's one. When I leave here this evening, I have to go home and cook. I hate to cook. I hate it with a passion, but it's just one of those things you have to do. I've done it every day for twenty years. I hate it, but you have to do certain things."

See, she wasn't cooking out of Divine Energy. She was doing it out of this other kind of consciousness. So I said to her, "Well, I'm hoping I can show you today a way of thinking and communicating that will help you get back in touch with your Divine Energy and make sure that you only come out of that. And you can then present things to others so that they can come out of that energy."

She was a rapid learner. She went home that very night and announced to her family that she no longer wanted to cook. And I got some feedback from her family. About three weeks later, who shows up at a training but her two older sons. They came up before the training and said to me, "We want to tell you how much change has occurred in our family since our mother came to your workshop."

I said, "Oh, yeah. You know, I've been very curious. She told me all the changes she's been making in her life, and I'm always wondering how that affects other family members. So I'm glad you guys showed up tonight. What was it like that first night when she came home and said she no longer wanted to cook?"

The oldest son said to me, "Marshall, I said to myself, 'Thank God. Now maybe she won't complain after every meal.'"

Q: HOW CAN I TELL WHEN I'M CONNECTING TO WHAT'S ALIVE IN SOMEONE ELSE?

A: When we do things that don't come out of this Divine Energy in each of us, this Divine Energy that makes compassionate giving natural—when we come out of any culturally learned pattern of doing things because we should, have to, must, out of guilt, out of shame, duty, obligation, or to get rewards—that is when *everybody* pays for it. Nonviolent Communication wants us to be clear, to not respond unless our response is coming out of this Divine Energy. And you'll know it is when you are willing to do what is requested. Even if it's hard work, it will be joyful if your only motive is to make life more wonderful.

When we put this all together, it looks like this: We may start a dialogue with other people by telling them what's alive in us and what we would like them to do to make life more wonderful for us. Then no matter how they respond, we try to connect with what's alive in them and what would make life more wonderful for them. We keep this flow of communication going until we find strategies to meet everybody's needs, and we want to always be sure that whatever strategies people agree to, they're agreeing freely, out of a willing desire to contribute to the well-being of one another.

Q: CAN YOU GIVE ANOTHER EXAMPLE OF HOW YOU'VE ACTUALLY USED THIS PROCESS TO CONNECT WITH OTHERS?

A: I was working in a refugee camp in a country not very pleased with the United States. There were about a hundred and seventy people assembled, and when my interpreter announced that I was an American citizen, one of the people jumped up and screamed at me, "Murderer." I was glad I knew Nonviolent Communication that day. It enabled me to see the beauty behind that person's message, what was alive and human in him. We do that in Nonviolent Communication by hearing the feelings and needs behind any message.

So I said to this gentleman, "Are you feeling angry because your need for support isn't getting met by my country?" Now, that required me to try to sense what he was feeling and needing. I could have been wrong. But even if we are wrong, if we are sincerely trying to connect with the Divine Energy in other human beings—their feelings, their needs at that moment—that shows them that no matter how they communicate with us, we care about what's alive in them. And when a person trusts that, we're well on our way to making a connection in which everybody's needs can get met. But it didn't happen right away, because this gentleman was in a lot of pain.

However, it happened that I guessed right, because when I said, "Are you angry because your need for support isn't being met by my country?" he said, "You're darn right." And he added to that, "We don't have sewage systems. We don't have housing. Why are you sending your weapons?"

So I said, "So, sir, if I'm hearing you again, you're saying that it's very painful when you need things like sewage systems and you need things like housing, and when weapons are sent instead; it's very painful."

He said, "Of course. Do you know what it's like to live under these conditions for twenty-eight years?"

"So, sir, you're saying that it's very painful, and you need some understanding for the conditions that you're living under." An hour later, the gentleman invited me to a Ramadan dinner at his house.

This is what happens when we can connect with what's alive in us, the humanness in one another, the feelings and needs behind any message. This doesn't mean we always have to say it out loud. Sometimes it's pretty obvious what people are feeling and needing; we don't have to say it. They'll feel it from our eyes whether we are really trying to connect with them.

Notice this does not require that we agree with everyone. It doesn't mean we have to like what they're saying. It means that we give them this precious gift of our presence, to be present at this moment to what's alive in them and that we are interested in that, sincerely interested—not as a psychological technique, but because we want to connect with the Divine Energy in them at this moment.

Q: THE PROCESS OF CONNECTING TO THE DIVINE ENERGY IN OTHERS WITH NVC SEEMS CLEAR ENOUGH ON PAPER, BUT ISN'T IT HARD TO ACTUALLY LIVE BY?

A: Just about everybody that studies Nonviolent Communication says two things about it. First, they say how easy it is—I mean, how simple. Just the two questions, and all we have to do is keep our communication, our focus of attention, our consciousness on what's alive in us and on what would make life more wonderful. How simple. The second thing they say about it is how difficult it is. Now, how can something be so simple and so difficult at the same time?

It's difficult because we haven't been taught to think about what's alive in us. We have been educated to fit under structures in which a few people dominate many. We have been taught to pay the most attention to what people—especially the authorities—think of us. We know that if they judge us as bad, wrong, incompetent, stupid, lazy, selfish, we're going to get punished. And if they label us as good or bad little boys and girls, good or bad employees, then we will be rewarded or punished. So we haven't been educated to think in terms of what's alive in us and what would make life more wonderful.

Nonviolent Communication suggests that we let people know what's alive in us in relationship to what they're doing. We want to be honest in Nonviolent Communication, but we want to be honest without using any words that imply enemy images, wrongness, criticism, insults, and psychological diagnosis.

Many people believe that you just can't do this with some people. They believe that some people are so damaged that no matter what communication you use, you're not going to arrive at this point. That has not been my experience. It just might take some time. Like when I'm working in one of the various prisons throughout the world. I'm not saying that this connection can happen right away; it may take quite awhile for people being punished for a crime to really trust that I'm sincerely interested in what's alive in them. Sometimes it's not easy to stay with that, because my own cultural conditioning didn't allow me to be fluent at this earlier in my life; so learning this can be a real challenge.

Q: HOW DO YOU GET ENEMIES TO RECOGNIZE THE DIVINE IN EACH OTHER?

A: When you get people connected at the level of Divine Energy, it's hard to maintain those "enemy" images. Nonviolent Communication, in its purity, is the most powerful, quickest way I've found to get people to go from life-alienated ways of thinking, where they want to hurt each other, to enjoying giving to each other.

When I have had a couple of people facing each other, Hutu and Tutsi, and their families have been killed by each other, it's amazing that in two or three hours we can get them nurturing each other. It's inevitable—*inevitable.* That's why I use this approach.

Given the amount of suffering that has gone on, it amazes me how simple it is and how quickly it can happen. Nonviolent Communication really quickly heals people who have experienced a lot of pain. This motivates me to want to make it happen even more quickly, because the way we're doing it now, with just a few people at a time, still takes awhile.

How do we get this done more quickly with the other eight hundred thousand Hutus and Tutsis who didn't come to our training, and with the rest of the planet? I would like to explore what would happen if we could make movies or television shows of this process, because I've seen that when two people go through the process with other people watching, vicarious learning, healing, and reconciliations happen. I would like to explore ways to use the media to get masses of people to go quickly through this process together.

Q: HOW BASIC IS OUR NEED TO GIVE TO ONE ANOTHER?

A: I think the need to enrich life is one of the most basic and powerful needs we all have. Another way to say this is that we need to act from the Divine Energy within us. And I think that when we *are* that Divine Energy, there is nothing we like more—nothing in which we find more joy—than enriching life, than using our immense power to enrich life.

But whenever we are trying to meet this need of ours to live this Divine Energy, trying to contribute to life, there is also another need and a request that goes with it. We have a need for information, and so we make a request for feedback from the person whose life we are trying to enrich. We want to know, "Is my intention being fulfilled by my action? Was my attempt to contribute successful?"

In our culture, that request gets distorted into our thinking that we have a *need* for the other person to love us for what we've done, to appreciate what we've done, to approve of us for what we've done. And that distorts and screws up the beauty of the whole process. It wasn't the other person's approval that we needed. Our very intent was to use our energy to enrich life. But we need the feedback. How do I know my effort was successful unless I get feedback?

And I can use this feedback to help me know if I am coming out of Divine Energy. I know that I am coming out of Divine Energy when I am able to value a criticism as much as a thank you.

Q: HAVE YOU ENCOUNTERED ANY CULTURAL OR LANGUAGE BARRIERS TO THIS PROCESS?

A: It amazes me how few and how little they are. When I first started to teach this process in another language, I really doubted that it could be done. I remember the first time I was in Europe; I was going to go first to Munich and then to Geneva. My colleague and I both doubted that we could get this through in another language. She was going to do it in French, and I would be there for her to ask me questions if something came up. I was going to at least try to see if we could go through translators. But it worked so well without any problems, and I find the same thing everywhere.

So I just don't worry about it. I'll do it in English, and you translate it, and it works very well. I can't think of any culture in which we've had any problem other than little things, but not with the essence of it. Not only have we had no problems, but also repeatedly, after trainings all over the world, a variety of people tell me that this is essentially what their religion says. It's old stuff; they know this stuff, and they're grateful for this manifestation. But it's nothing new.

Q: DO YOU BELIEVE A SPIRITUAL PRACTICE IS IMPORTANT FOR PRACTICING NONVIOLENCE?

A: I recommend in all workshops that people take time to ask themselves this question, "How do I choose to connect with other human beings?" and to be as conscious as they can about that—to make sure it's their choice and not the way they've been programmed to choose. Really, what is the way you would choose to connect with other human beings?

Gratitude also plays a big role for me. If I am conscious of a human act that I want to express gratitude for, conscious of how I feel when the act occurs—whether it's my act or someone else's, and regardless of what needs of mine it fulfills—then expressing gratitude fills me with consciousness of the power that we human beings have to enrich lives. It makes me aware that we are Divine Energy, that we have such power to make life wonderful, and that there is nothing we like better than to do just that.

To me, that is powerful evidence of our Divine Energy, that we have this power to make life so wonderful, and that there is nothing we like more. That's why part of my spiritual practice is to be conscious of gratitude and expressing gratitude.

Q: HAVE YOU BEEN INFLUENCED BY PAST MOVEMENTS THAT HAVE ATTEMPTED TO MEDIATE BETWEEN SPIRITUALITY AND SOCIAL CHANGE, LIKE THOSE OF GANDHI OR MARTIN LUTHER KING JR.?

A: Well, I certainly have been affected by them, because I've studied people historically who were getting things done in a way that I value, and they certainly are two people who were doing that. The kind of spirituality I value is one in which you get great joy out of contributing to life, not just sitting and meditating, although meditation is certainly valuable. But, from the meditation, from the resulting consciousness, I would like to see people in action, creating the world they want to live in.

RECOMMENDED READING

Nonviolent Communication: A Language of Life, 2nd Ed. by Marshall B. Rosenberg, PhD

Speak Peace in a World of Conflict by Marshall B. Rosenberg, PhD

The Open and Closed Mind: Investigations into the Nature of Belief Systems and Personality Systems by Milton Rokeach

The Powers That Be: Theology for a New Millennium by Walter Wink

Spirit Matters by Michael Lerner

A Spirituality of Resistance: Finding a Peaceful Heart and Protecting the Earth by Roger S. Gottlieb

ABOUT THE CENTER FOR NONVIOLENT COMMUNICATION

The Center for Nonviolent Communication (CNVC) is an international nonprofit peacemaking organization with the vision of a world in which everyone's needs are met peacefully. CNVC is devoted to supporting the spread of Nonviolent Communication (NVC) around the world.

Founded in 1984 by Dr. Marshall B. Rosenberg, CNVC has been contributing to a vast social transformation in thinking, speaking, and acting—showing people how to connect in ways that inspire compassionate results. NVC is now being taught around the globe in communities, schools, prisons, mediation centers, churches, businesses, professional conferences, and more. More than two hundred certified trainers and hundreds more teach NVC to approximately 250,000 people each year in thirty-five countries.

CNVC believes that NVC training is a crucial step in continuing to build a compassionate, peaceful society. Your tax-deductible donation will help CNVC continue to provide training in some of the most impoverished, violent corners of the world. It will also support the development and continuation of organized projects aimed at bringing NVC training to high-need geographic regions and populations.

To make a tax-deductible donation or to learn more about the valuable resources described below, visit the CNVC website at cnvc.org:

- **Training and Certification:** Find local, national, and international training opportunities; access trainer certification information; and connect to local NVC communities, trainers, and more.
- **CNVC Bookstore:** Find mail- or phone-order information for a complete selection of NVC books, booklets, and audio and video materials.
- **CNVC Projects:** Seven regional and theme-based projects provide focus and leadership for teaching NVC in a particular application or geographic region.
- **E-Groups and LISTSERVS™:** Join one of several moderated, topic-based NVC e-groups and LISTSERVS developed to support individual learning and the continued growth of NVC worldwide.

For more information, please contact CNVC at 5600-A San Francisco Road NE, Albuquerque, NM 87109; phone: 505-244-4041; fax: 505-247-0414; email: cnvc@cnvc.org; website: cnvc.org

AN INVITATION

What's missing from this transcription is the experience of sharing time and space with Marshall Rosenberg or one of the CNVC certified trainers. The power, warmth, and poignancy of the NVC message are amplified by being at a training session in person. The interplay with a live audience adds a dimension to the learning process that is hard to match on paper. If you'd like to see Marshall or another CNVC trainer in person, please visit cnvc.org for a schedule of NVC trainings and speaking engagements, as well as a listing of NVC trainers and support people around the world.

For a listing of NVC materials—audios, CDs, books, and more—please visit cnvc.org. For additional NVC books and publication information, please visit NonviolentCommunication.com.

ABOUT THE AUTHOR

Marshall B. Rosenberg, PhD, is the founder and director of educational services for the Center for Nonviolent Communication (CNVC), an international peacemaking organization. He is the author of *Speak Peace in a World of Conflict* and the best-selling *Nonviolent Communication: A Language of Life*. Marshall is the proud recipient of the 2006 Global Village Foundation's Bridge of Peace Award and the Association of Unity Churches International 2006 Light of God Expressing in Society Award.

Growing up in a turbulent Detroit neighborhood, Marshall developed a keen interest in new forms of communication that would provide peaceful alternatives to the violence he encountered. His interest led to a doctorate in clinical psychology from the University of Wisconsin in 1961, where he studied under Carl Rogers. His subsequent life experience and study of comparative religion motivated him to develop the NVC process.

Marshall first used the NVC process in federally funded school integration projects during the 1960s to provide mediation and communication skills training. In 1984 he founded CNVC, which is now affiliated with more than two hundred certified NVC trainers in thirty-five countries around the globe.

AWARDS

2006: Bridge of Peace Award from the Global Village Foundation

2006: Light of God Expressing in Society Award from the Association of Unity Churches International

2004: Religious Science International Golden Works Award

2004: International Peace Prayer Day Man of Peace Award by the Healthy, Happy Holy Organization (3HO)

2002: Princess Anne of England and Chief of Police Restorative Justice Appreciation Award

2000: International Listening Association Listener of the Year Award

With guitar and puppets in hand, a history of traveling to some of the most violent corners of the world, and a spiritual energy that fills a room, Marshall shows us how to create a more peaceful and satisfying world. Marshall is currently based in Albuquerque, New Mexico. For bonus content from this author, please visit SoundsTrue.com/bonus/LivingNVC.

ABOUT SOUNDS TRUE

Sounds True is a multimedia publisher whose mission is to inspire and support personal transformation and spiritual awakening. Founded in 1985 and located in Boulder, Colorado, we work with many of the leading spiritual teachers, thinkers, healers, and visionary artists of our time. We strive with every title to preserve the essential "living wisdom" of the author or artist. It is our goal to create products that not only provide information to a reader or listener but that also embody the quality of a wisdom transmission.

For those seeking genuine transformation, Sounds True is your trusted partner. At SoundsTrue.com you will find a wealth of free resources to support your journey, including exclusive weekly audio interviews, free downloads, interactive learning tools, and other special savings on all our titles.

For two free downloads, please visit SoundsTrue.com/bonus/free_gifts.

many voices, one journey